THE MORTGAGE CODE

HELPING YOU MOVE UP THE PROPERTY LADDER, GET THE BEST MORTGAGE, AVOID COSTLY MISTAKES, AND SAVE MONEY

ANGELA CALLA

LIONCREST
PUBLISHING

THE MORTGAGE CODE

Helping You Move Up the Property Ladder, Get the Best Mortgage, Avoid Costly Mistakes, and Save Money

ISBN   978-1-5445-1204-4 *Paperback*

978-1-5445-1203-7 *Ebook*

978-1-5445-1205-1 *Audiobook*

CONTENTS

FOREWORD

BY GARY MAURIS

It was a grey, rainy day the first time I met Angela Calla. I had heard a lot about this young go-getter from her boyfriend and eventual husband, Rob.

I was studying for my mortgage broker licence in our local library, when Rob—who was studying for his real estate licence—began telling me about this woman who had, less than a year before, passed her mortgage exam. He spoke about her as if she were something magical. He said, "You've got to meet her, she's as sharp as a tack and super-high energy; she is going places! You two will totally click!"

We were just launching what would eventually become Canada's National Mortgage Company. Over the next twelve years, Dominion Lending Centres did in fact become the most recognizable and dominant mortgage originator in Canada. Today, the DLC Group funds over $40 billion of mortgages every year, via more than 6,000 mortgage professionals enjoying a colossal market share of more than 40 percent.

At the very young age of twenty-three, Angela was ready to take on the world, convinced that nothing would stand in her way. I delighted that she was willing to leave her current mortgage company and join a new and unproven start-up like mine. We both took a chance on each other that day, and, all these years later, I still am glad we did.

What I didn't realize at the time was what good instincts Angela had. She would prove over and over that she has a keen eye for recognizing opportunities and was willing to take a chance and jump on anything she believed in, regardless of the challenge.

She's always had one speed: fast! She joined me with no fallback, no life preserver; she had to be successful, and she didn't disappoint. The very first year, she became one of our top brokers and she has been at the very top of the industry since then. It's not like she didn't have competition, either: Dominion Lending Centres became a powerhouse in Canada and most of the top brokers in the country are licensed with us, so to see her excel in that environment says everything.

Although I've always been in awe of Angela's drive and of her get-it-done attitude, two things really stand out about her:

She has always taken her profession life-threateningly seriously. She could have started coasting a long time ago. Today, she is financially independent and has many investments, including multiple properties, but doesn't stop. She has an insatiable desire to learn and she constantly invests in herself. She always knows exactly what's going on and what's new in the world of finance, and she is sharp and ready to be called anytime by the media and be the authority on the Canadian housing and mortgage market.

She doesn't get rattled and continues to be incredibly dependable even with anything that life throws at her, including aging parents, erratic and changing mortgage rules, and the chaos that operating at that high level often brings with it.

Her motto, "Count on Calla," started out tongue-in-cheek, but it's become completely accurate and describes her and how she lives her life. My office has been next to hers for twelve years, during which time I've witnessed firsthand how she seemingly effortlessly continues to create a beautiful family with her husband and two amazing kids, while balancing a busy career as a media personality, personal finance guru, and top mortgage professional assisting thousands of clients. As CEO, I personally refer many mortgage clients to Angela: I know I can always "count on Calla" to take amazing care of my family and friends.

I know Angela's next ten years will be her best ten years—if that's even possible.

Congrats, Angela!

GARY MAURIS

PRESIDENT, DOMINION LENDING CENTRES

INTRODUCTION

Getting the best mortgage is about more than shopping for the lowest rate, worrying about points, or comparing which company offers the best incentives. Getting the best mortgage involves understanding what I call The Mortgage Code.

How, do you ask? As when understanding anything, the key to cracking the code is to develop intelligence. I'll start with an analogy: if we can say that *knowledge* is understanding that a tomato is a fruit, then *intelligence* means knowing not to put that tomato into a fruit salad!

Having knowledge doesn't mean you also have the ability to execute it intelligently. Intelligence comes from understanding different levels of knowledge, then having the support to strategically execute that knowledge for best results. It means having the ability to understand both sides of any question.

The truth is that nobody really understands mortgages. There are reasons for that: mortgages are complicated, and lenders don't do much to demystify them. To the contrary, lenders[1] have known for decades (and take advantage of the fact) that most people are exhausted. We're all tired: we get up, we go to work, we try to eat right, we raise our kids in the best way we can—and after all that, what we crave is simplicity. As a result, lenders give clients one simple thing to review.

That one simple thing—marketed by lenders to borrowers for decades—is the interest rate.

Yet oddly enough, the interest rate is not the most significant contributing factor to what you pay on a mortgage—a subject we'll talk more about shortly. In fact, I'm going to share information with you that you've probably never thought about, things people who aren't in the business just don't know.

Because of their overall exhaustion, people look for the easiest way out. Give them a canned answer, and chances are they'll follow that advice. "Want to get preapproved in sixty seconds? Step right this way..." No one has time to think anymore, and as a result, people are paying far too much for their mortgages. What I hope to do with this

---

1   When we talk about "lenders," the term can include anyone who actually finances the mortgage: banks, credit unions, insurance companies, monoline lenders, trust companies, etc.

book is get you to stop and think. To assess what marketers are trying to sell you and why. To figure out what is being omitted from their "best offers."

The best mortgage strategy lies in proactive ways of thinking and in understanding what's important when weighing several options. What I'll tell you now—and what I'll continue to tell you throughout this book—is that everyone's asking the wrong question. They're asking, "What's the interest rate?" when they should be asking, "What is this going to cost me based on the terms?"

I can gauge someone's level of mortgage intelligence based on the first two seconds of the phone call. If the caller asks, "What's the interest rate?" I know right away there's going to be some education involved in this process. We're going to have to start with the basics. And that's fine because I want people to really understand what is happening; I want to save them money, and becoming educated about the process will invariably save money.

On the other hand, if the caller asks, "How do I get the best mortgage?" I know their level of mortgage intelligence is significantly higher right out of the gate, and we can get to the meat and potatoes a lot quicker. This caller hasn't been brainwashed by marketing and is looking to deploy significant intelligence.

Gaining that intelligence is the first thing I need you to learn. Beyond that, my hope is that you'll learn the importance of aligning yourself with the right people. What we're discussing here is mortgages, but the questions I want you to ask are applicable in the context of any product. These questions will help you dig deeper into what you're not being told. That's when you get the best results.

We'll start with one statement of fact: it's impossible to shop intelligently for a mortgage on your own. Two mortgage offers might read the same way, but the history of the lender and what the product actually means to that lender are two different things. If everybody valued the same things equally, we would all go on the same vacation. If everybody valued the same things equally, we would all just marry whoever asked us. If everyone just wanted the lowest-cost car, everyone would end up with a Ford Pinto.

Think about aging for a moment. I use a different beauty routine and face cream than I did when I was in my teens and twenties. I had two back-to-back pregnancies, was breastfeeding, doing a weekly radio show, managing a team, running a business...it all catches up to your face! I adapt; we all have to adapt. We don't all value the same things equally, or even value the same things at different points in our lives.

When I booked my first recurring spot as a mortgage educator on a former local realty show that ran on City TV, I decided to buy myself a used two-seater soft-top convertible BMW Z3. I was in my early twenties and single: it seemed like an awesome ride, right? I know my friends sure loved it, especially the ones who got to ride with me! Fast-forward a few years: I got married and then later was pregnant with my first child, and I thought, Uh, yeah, this vehicle won't work anymore; I can't put a car seat in it, and we won't be able to go anywhere as a family. While I was pregnant and spring was approaching, I took the opportunity to sell that car and get a safer family vehicle. It was the right thing to do for the right season of our lives. In the same way, your life stage, your goals, your family life, and your responsibilities and priorities will always be key factors in your decision and life-modifying options moving forward. A mortgage is no different!

Every situation carries different meanings for different people. The right mortgage for you depends on a number of factors: your lifestyle, your values, and your life stage. It depends on what you can and cannot control. Working through all of those options and then being able to quickly shift in a changing market or lifestyle are the keys to success.

I want you to understand your responsibilities, what the mortgage process entails, and what you can and can't control. I want you to be ready for what is ahead of you:

the responsibilities of being a homeowner and paying a mortgage. I also want you to see the opportunities your mortgage will create for you when you execute it intelligently and with the right people.

WHAT YOU'RE DOING WRONG

Myths and misconceptions can lead to costly mistakes.

Most people are loyal to the bank they use. They know the tellers; they may be friendly with the bank manager; it's a familiar place. The assumption most people make is that since you've been a loyal customer for a certain number of years, your bank will go out of its way to treat you well and offer you the best mortgage product available. But that's simply not the case.

The bank is a revolving door. On average, people work between two and five years in any given bank position. Think about who moves up in any bank: it's the people who make the bank the most money, not the people who save you the most money. The banks reward the employees who sell the most.

There are two completely different goals here. *Your* goal is to get the best possible mortgage for your situation and save money. Your *bank's* goal is to make money for its shareholders. It is that simple, that black and white.

The nice, friendly people who work at your bank are getting paid to sell their product. Their income is based on what they can sell and how many cross-sale opportunities are available within the institution. Once you realize that, you also realize they cannot have your best interests in mind. Of course they're going to give you their best product whenever possible, but they're simply not in a position to tell you if there's something better out there. That's not available to them.

Here's another way of looking at it: imagine the last time you went to McDonald's and the person at the counter said, "Hey, you know what? Our beef isn't that good today. You should go to A&W instead."

Right? That just doesn't happen.

Let's consider some of the terms you might be offered. Here's an example: "To get out of this mortgage entails three months' interest, or the interest rate differential." That's fine, but it doesn't tell you how they're going to calculate their interest rate, does it? Besides that, lenders can modify their interest rates on a daily basis.

That's right: posted rates can be modified daily, and that's completely out of your control. A good place to start is looking at lenders who only have fully discounted rates. In that case, you know what you're going to get all the time. It's consistent, and you know it's going to be lower than someone who has posted rates.

I'm not saying banks are evil, or wrong, or anything like that. Banks can give you a good deal. We work with banks when the right product fits one of our clients' needs. Occasionally, there will be someone who needs to meet targets, and that person might be able to do something that wouldn't generally be possible with multiple levels of compliance. Just remember one thing: by the time anything negative happens, that person isn't going to be the one dealing with it. They'll be long gone from that position.

In general, lenders tend to be reactive, not proactive. Ask yourself this: when was the last time your lender contacted you to show you how to save money—even if doing so meant they'd make less? When does that happen? Never. There has to be someone else in between who's looking out for your interests, and that's where a first-rate mortgage team comes in. In any industry, it's who you align yourself with that makes all the difference.

It's essential for you to understand that banks have a unique (and not particularly client-centred) perspective on mortgages. Banks exist to cross-sell, to make and retain money—and the people who move up within the bank's hierarchy are the people who make the most money for the bank. They are certainly not the people who save the most amount of money for the client. Again, ask yourself: When was the last time my bank contacted me to offer me a way to save money?

Look at the promotions most banks run. "Open up an account with us, and we'll give you something," or "Do a mortgage with us and get a free iPad," or "Get free chequing for two years." Wait. They're making all these offers to people who aren't even their clients! Does that make sense? Why show loyalty to an institution that would never show you loyalty in return? Why align yourself with a bank offering all the bells and whistles to new people, but treating existing clients like second-class citizens? We do the opposite: we always make the best offers to existing clients before we offer something like that to a new one.

Once you analyze them, the offers aren't even that attractive. Someone new coming in the door is going to get all these perks, but you can be sure the bank doesn't plan to lose money on that new client: they're going to make up for those newcomer packages somewhere along the line. Maybe they'll raise their rates over the next few years to cover what they offered as a lure. Or maybe the terms of their mortgages aren't all that great, and what they've done is offer a distraction, a psychological play. They know people want an easy reason to say yes.

And it works. The parent who's blowing bubbles to distract

the child getting an immunization knows it works. The nurse who gives the child a sticker after they've put on a Band-Aid knows it works. This is no different: the bank knows a good distraction works, too.

The real takeaways here are straightforward: not all mortgages are the same, and your bank doesn't have your back.

COSTLY MISTAKES

Selecting your mortgage broker is one of the most important financial decisions you'll ever make. This is where my company is different from all the others: we are here to do the best for our client, even when the best thing for them is to not do business with us right now. I can't speak for every mortgage provider in the country, but what I can say is that's our core value. Helping our clients find the right mortgage at the right time is what leads and informs what we do.

Choosing a mortgage based on rate alone is like buying a car strictly on price. Imagine this: You see a car advertised in the newspaper for an extremely low price. Without looking at its features, you buy the car and bring it home only to realize that it doesn't have a radio, air conditioning, or power steering, and has over 200,000 kilometres on it.

No one would buy a car without looking at the list of features first. You can't test-drive a mortgage; all you can do is read the fine print!

Most people are unaware of how much damage taking out the wrong mortgage can do to them. A woman came in recently for a consultation. She'd received a mortgage on her own, and the lender had failed to disclose that their terrific low rate came with a sale-only clause. Now she's paying tens of thousands of dollars more than she should in interest payments because she can't refinance her mortgage early to include her outside debt and pay her outstanding taxes. She's stuck with the original mortgage terms for another three years.

She wasn't told when she was getting this "excellent low-rate mortgage" that she'd be stuck with it until she sold. That kind of mortgage would have been fine if she'd wanted to sell, but she didn't. Some people want to stay in their homes on their terms. Why should you have to sell in order to access your equity?

Did the person offering her that mortgage care? Of course not. They had targets to make. What if she'd discovered the clause later and wanted to talk to the representative about it? She would have been out of luck, because that representative would have moved on. I can't tell you how often we hear stories like this one. I feel sorry for these people and the situations in which they find themselves.

And there's the real problem: she didn't take the time to align herself with the right company, and she paid the price—both figuratively and literally.

What you might not know is that seven out of ten mortgages are broken between twenty-four and thirty-eight months in. If you think you're not going to have any changes in your needs or life situation over the next five years, you have a 70 percent chance of being wrong.

When you know better, you do better. When you work with an independent mortgage professional you won't have any unanswered questions. There isn't anything hidden anywhere. We go through all the options available to you.

The biggest mistake people make, and I will go back to this again and again, is that they don't understand the difference between the interest they pay and the interest rate. If you ask for rates, you're going to be sold a bill of goods from someone who's offering what you perceive to be a favourable rate.

It's not the rate you should be asking about.

As we continue on this journey together, I hope you'll learn the importance of what I call the two Ps of the mortgage code: prepayment and penalties. Those are what you should be asking about.

When you understand true value, you understand it's the price you pay that matters, not the rate you receive. Unfortunately, most people don't even know they should ask the question. If someone walks into a bank and says, "I'm concerned about the rate I'll be paying," then of course that's the question the mortgage salesperson is going to answer. That's just basic sales training. If you ask the average banker what indicators they're watching to determine the mortgage strategy that's best for you, you're going to get a blank look...and then you're often going to get the wrong answer.

You have to think about exactly what it is you're asking. If you ask a lender, "If I take a fixed rate, am I protected against payment shock?" and they answer yes, they're wrong. It's that simple. Payment shock happens when a homeowner's monthly payments increase, and a fixed rate doesn't mean you're protected against future payment shock. You have to make optimal increases on that mortgage over time in order to protect yourself from future payment shock, and that can only happen in an environment where someone's proactively contacting you and letting you know what that number is in order to get ahead. You're not protected against anything in the mortgage market—even if you have a fixed closed interest rate. Asking the right questions makes all the difference, and you can be sure that an excellent mortgage professional knows which questions to ask.

SETTING EXPECTATIONS

Every profession has a process. Accessing a great mortgage professional is like having a great doctor. When you have a great doctor, you don't need to go to a walk-in clinic, because you know your own doctor will give you the best information suited for your specific long-term health plan. They're going to take everything into consideration.

Sometimes, though, you *do* have to use a walk-in clinic. And when that happens, you don't just walk through and see the medical professional. You check in first with reception, where they'll ask you what the problem is, the reason you're there. Why? Because the doctor needs to know everything in order to help you. If you go to a dentist, there's a similar preparedness: they have your chart handy, your x-rays, and your history, so they can help you.

In all of these scenarios, there's a process in place that enables the professionals to do their job and provide the best possible outcome for their patient. These processes have been tested and honed and proven to work.

We all accept these processes in the medical field. You wouldn't go to a general practitioner for heart surgery, would you? Your trusted GP is going to refer you to a surgeon, and you'll also probably do your own research to find the surgeon who's best aligned with your health goals. Once you've found that surgeon, you'll trust them to do what they do best and be confident they'll collaborate with you to accomplish your goal. You'll trust your dentist to refer you to an orthodontist or oral surgeon, because they have years of experience knowing who will be the right fit for your particular situation and needs.

Why would a mortgage expert be any different? We, too, have a process that's been tested and shown to be successful, so we can work together for the best possible outcome for our clients. We, too, have resources that we can align with your goals and needs.

When it comes to working toward your financial goals, why would you go to a lender—the financial equivalent of the general practitioner—when you could do your research and find the mortgage professional who is the best in their field?

You'd be surprised at the number of people we hear saying, "Just give me your best rate, because I know I have terrific credit and I have an amazing income." It doesn't work like that. There is a plethora of factors involved, so as your mortgage professional, I'm going to invest time, expertise, and the costs associated with reviewing your documents to do it right. If we can help you, my team will sit down with you and go over your options. If we can't help you, we'll explain what the process is, what plan we can put in place to modify your situation, and when we can review it again.

We don't just say no; we help you get from there to where you want to be. If that means we're not going to do business with you right now, we'll tell you so. We're making an investment in our future together, and we'll give you an honest answer. Maybe that honest answer is that you should sell your home. Maybe that honest answer is that you should consider filing bankruptcy. Whatever that scenario is—even if it doesn't benefit us financially— we're always led by our core values to do the best thing for our client.

TRANSPARENCY

Great mortgage professionals don't take shortcuts, and they have expectations of clients. We're going to send you a list of what we need, and we need that list in its entirety to review your options. We can't work together if you're not willing to give us what we need to help you.

Let's go back to the medical analogy for a moment. You have to be honest with your doctor, or they won't be able to help you. If you go to your doctor with a rash and you've been self-medicating with a topical cream, you have to share that information. If you're not honest with the doctor, then how can they give you the best treatment available?

The same goes for your mortgage. If you've shopped your

mortgage around and don't tell us, it's going to hurt your ability to move forward, and it's going to hurt how available lenders review you and your file. If you've gone to another mortgage broker who's not as experienced and you've submitted your file elsewhere, lenders are going to see that—and there's a good chance your application will be tagged as fraudulent.

An excellent team is going to expect transparency. They'll expect that they're the only people working on your file in order to do the best job for you. Lenders do the best for the top mortgage brokers; in our case, they give us new and exciting opportunities for our clients, and they do that because they know the expectations we have of our clients. If we have all the correct documents and submit them to our lenders in one fell swoop, our lenders can provide us with faster, more efficient approvals.

Setting expectations is one of the reasons we've been so successful. It has to do with what we want from, and for, our clients. The way we position a client is equally important to the client getting an approval—and not just any approval, but the absolute best approval. There's strategy behind everything we do so that our clients can be successful.

We had a self-employed graphic designer come to us for a mortgage, and I gave him a list of documents I'd need from him. He seemed bemused. "My bank just said I was approved," he said. I was astonished. How could they say he was approved without doing a full review? That sounds like a recipe for disaster. I turned the situation around for him: "What if I came to you and asked you to design me a logo, but you didn't take the time to interview me about the core values of my company, what's important to me, and what I am looking to portray. Could you possibly create the best logo for me? How could you?"

It was his "aha" moment. I could almost see the light bulb go on over his head. When it's put in those terms, anyone would say, "Oh that's obvious," but the trouble is they don't see it as being obvious in the mortgage sector. I find that inexplicable.

DOCUMENTATION DO'S AND DON'TS

The most common forms of income documentation we need are letters of employment and pay stubs, and it's important to understand right away that both of these documents have a shelf life of thirty days. We also need notices of assessment that show a zero balance, and we need T1s and T4s.[2]

When we ask for these documents, we need them in full. Don't send us your work contract and say it's your letter of employment. A work contract is a work contract; it's not a letter of employment.

When it comes to requiring things like T1 Generals, we need official company documents and financial statements if people are self-employed. We don't want you to pull your financials off QuickBooks. And, while we don't want fewer documents than what we request, we also don't want more. Don't send us things we don't ask for because that takes time. Legally, we have to process everything you send us: we have to review it—and destroy it if it's not applicable. When you give us too much ancillary documentation, you're taking time away from us being able to do what we do best.

We're going to ask you for specific information. If you have a question about whether something will assist your file, it's fine to ask us—but don't just send it. Don't ever send us anything with blacked-out areas or any paperwork that doesn't have your name on it. That won't meet

2   The T1 General (entitled Income Tax and Benefit Return) is the form used in Canada by individuals to file their personal income tax return. The US equivalent is the Form 1040. The T4 is a Canadian employer's form indicating salaried workers' income. The US equivalent is the Form W-2.

compliance and we'll just have to come back to you and request the whole document, and nobody is getting the result they want.

You'd be amazed at the number of people who feel a need to question the process. They may say, "I don't understand why. Why do you need this? I don't want to give it to you." As you can imagine, it's impossible to work in that kind of atmosphere of mistrust.

MOVING UP THE PROPERTY LADDER

In general, people start with the home they can afford, which isn't always the home they want. But as you build equity in your property, and your income changes, you can move up into a more suitable place. Moving up the property ladder takes an analysis of your current scenario, including your current mortgage, current equity, existing debt, existing income, and credit. Once you have the analysis, you need to develop a strategy.

Depending on your current mortgage, there might be a specific time that's best for you to make a move. Your income scenario and your credit may also dictate when is the optimal moment.

Finally, what you've done between when you first took out the mortgage and now is going to be a *major* factor.

If you bought a condo, then six months later took out a car loan for $800 a month, and then used your $10,000 line of credit to renovate your condo, these factors are going to make a difference in qualifying for a new mortgage. Believe it or not, that monthly $800 car payment, along with the monthly $300 credit payment, just removed $300,000 in mortgage qualification. Before you can qualify to buy another home, you'll have to pay that debt out by refinancing your existing home to consolidate the debt or through making more money or selling an asset.

When you're planning to move, you have to make sure everything else is in order first. Sometimes that means doing things in stages. We helped one couple—a social worker and a school principal—who started out not knowing what to do; they didn't understand the potential impact of their actions. As soon as they bought their house, they went ahead and got lines of credit, credit cards, and vehicles, and the husband finished his MBA. They ended up with about $100,000 in debt to consolidate before they could qualify to move up the property ladder.

With all those factors considered, you can't just go ahead and list your home one day and feel carefree, thinking that you can get a mortgage easily because you already have one. Mortgage guidelines and qualifications change every day, and that changes how your situation will be viewed. That's why having a proactive mortgage strategy is key to being able to reach all your goals. When clients work with us, we're reviewing their mortgages on a consistent basis to ensure that the market, their lifestyle, and their home are always being optimally used. That way they can make these changes with a lot less delay because they're continually keeping on top of them.

What my team does is use one credit check to shop all the lenders. If an individual went from lender to lender to lender, points would be taken off their score every time they submitted documents, impacting the mortgage price.

When your lower credit score affects the price you pay, it's because varying interest rates are available based on your score, and rates are premiumed accordingly. If you've already gone to one of the lenders we may have sent your mortgage to, then you no longer qualify as a "new client." If they come up with a last-minute, quick-closing special or a special offer, you wouldn't qualify because you disqualified yourself by doing this on your own.

GETTING THE RIGHT ADVICE

I'm hoping that by now you're starting to understand that you won't get the best deal when you try and negotiate a mortgage on your own, with a bank, or with the wrong mortgage provider. It's not always apparent who the best professional might be, but here are four questions you should ask your mortgage provider to help you differentiate among them:

- **What do you base your mortgage rates on, and why?** This gauges the provider's mortgage intelligence. There's only one answer: fixed interest rates are based on the bond market, and variable interest rates are based on the Bank of Canada.[3] If the provider isn't watching the right market indicators, how could they possibly help you with the best mortgage?
- **Am I protected from changes in the mortgage market if I have a fixed rate?** The answer should be no. Nobody's protected. When you have a mortgage, you need to make consistent modifications in order to ensure you're optimizing the market and taking advantage of the current situation you're in. We have strategies that will keep you ahead of inflation and protect you from payment shock, and these strategies involve the client following our advice.
- **What strategy are you recommending, and why is it important?** This helps you gauge what they're doing, and their commitment level in proactively managing your mortgage. There have been enormous changes in the mortgage market since the Great Depression, but every moment creates its own opportunity. Regardless

---

3   The fixed-rate mortgage interest rate is compounded every six months in Canada, but not in the United States. In the US, the major factor influencing rates is the movement of the ten-year Treasury bond.

of what is happening, you need a strategy, so if your professional isn't approaching you to develop one and is just relying on interest rates, there's a problem.

- **What personal commitment do you have to your clients?** Does this broker have a proactive communication system? Do they review mortgages and contact you when some new development might work in your favour? I can guarantee one thing: if your mortgage isn't being reviewed, it's costing you money.

If you get a mortgage on your own, you'll find lenders are reactive. They'll send you a notice after the rates have gone up, when it's not particularly helpful. What are you supposed to do about it then? The increase has already happened.

Most lenders send you mortgage statements every year, but unless you walk into their office or call them, they're not going to do anything else for you: being proactive isn't to their advantage. What's advantageous to them is selling you mortgage products—and spending the fewest resources on you after that. Lenders will call you to sell you a credit card; they won't call you to make changes to your mortgage that will save you money.

And that's the true difference. Mortgage professionals like me want to save you money; in fact, I'm absolutely committed to saving you money. I keep helping clients review the market, not once or twice, but continually. Anytime there's a point-five percent difference in the mortgage market, you can be sure we're reviewing your mortgage to see how you can best optimize it. We know that regardless of where you are in your mortgage, there's always an opportunity to optimize it or protect yourself from what may be happening in the future.

DOING IT RIGHT

I'm thinking of a couple I worked with from Coquitlam, Danielle and Scott. She was a schoolteacher and he was a social worker. They were considering moving up the property ladder but weren't sure if they should wait until their mortgage renewal date.[4] They'd gotten a mortgage through a mortgage broker before, but after the mortgage completed, they hadn't heard back from that broker. They decided they needed guidance from someone else.

They were smart to review their options around choosing a mortgage professional. There's been tremendous change in the mortgage market over the last ten years. You can't just set up your mortgage and forget about it—there's an analogy here for all my foodie friends: this isn't Instapot cooking! When Danielle and Scott contacted us, they had a good mortgage, but they also had about $100,000 in

---

4   In Canada, mortgages are scheduled to come up for renewal; this isn't a factor in the U.S. mortgage market.

outside debt. Their idea was to wait until they sold their house to pay out that debt, and then move up the property ladder. What they didn't know was those payments were going to keep them from moving up the property ladder, and their credit score was negatively impacted by all those debts. By consolidating the debt, they were able to save $1,600 every month.

Within a year, their credit was much better and they qualified to buy their dream home. In other words, they moved up the property ladder. They had no idea their existing debt was impacting them because they weren't used to thinking like that. They were both high-income earners so didn't think there was a problem with carrying debt they knew they'd be able to eventually pay off. But once they acquired the necessary mortgage intelligence and worked with the right mortgage professionals, their lives improved substantially.

Not everybody gets it right, unfortunately. We followed up with another couple who had come to us inquiring about preapproval so they could buy a home, but they didn't follow through with sending us their documents. Then they made an offer on a home, the offer was accepted, and that's when they sent us the required documentation—marked "urgent," of course.

Things went downhill from there. It turned out they also

sent those documents to a bank and to another broker, without mentioning it to us. When we submitted their package to a lender, the lender red-flagged it. We'd pulled the credit report before the others had, so we weren't aware of any problem, but now the whole process halted because it was unclear who was working on the file or what exactly was going on. They ended up getting flagged for fraud and didn't get their approval in time, all simply because of a lack of transparency.

If we'd known they were shopping it, we would probably have declined the file in the first place. People coming to us and to mortgage professionals like us know the value we offer. They know our reputation and why we're doing what we're doing. If I don't feel someone's being honest with us, it's an immediate hint as to how the relationship will continue.

Other things can go wrong, of course. I mentioned another client, a couple who had a preapproval, and then—for reasons best known to themselves—bought a car and some furniture in the weeks that elapsed between the preapproval and the final approval. Most lenders pull a final credit score before physically approving the file, so when that happened, the client's score had dropped twenty points, disqualifying them from the rate we'd secured at the preapproval.

There are scenarios in which people just aren't going to

qualify based on certain circumstances, no matter whether those variables are self-inflicted or the result of fraud. It's not the end of the world. When they can't qualify, we show them what they can do to improve their chances. Some self-employed clients, for example, don't have the kind of paperwork favoured by traditional lenders, and we have a different set of lenders best for them. The interest rate is higher, and there will be fees, but the point is that we know where to go to give any client their best option.

Whatever the scenario, it's important to navigate the market and give clients clarity so they can make the best decision moving forward.

DON'T MAKE COMPARISONS

Everyone knows someone else who got a mortgage. Your parents got a mortgage, your colleague got a mortgage, your neighbour got a mortgage, and you saw how it worked for them. That's how it's going to work for you, right? Wrong. Everyone is different, and every day is different, too. Everything in the mortgage industry changes daily. Comparing yourself to others is a pointless and unfruitful exercise, period.

Yes, there was a time when you could get an equity lender. That time is not now. There was a time when you could just give a pay stub and get a mortgage. That time is not now. What happened in the past isn't relevant. What is relevant is what experts tell you about your particular scenario and your particular timing right at this moment.

The medical analogy holds true here, too. "My friend had this same cough, and she got better, so I want the same prescription you wrote for her." No. What worked for your friend might not work for you. It might even be harmful for you. You can't compare yourself to others. It's an exercise in futility.

MY JOURNEY AND SUCCESS

The reason I became a mortgage broker is a combination of two factors: my passion for real estate and investing and my core value system. I've always believed that people deserve to get the best and they shouldn't have to play a game to get what is right for them. I sincerely love to save people money. I want to help make their lives better. From the beginning, I saw mortgage advice as an opportunity to help normal people get ahead.

Back when I was in school, a teacher told me, "Hey, if you bring me one hundred dollars today, I'll guarantee you'll have a million by the time you're sixty-five." He didn't have to ask twice! I brought him the hundred dollars the next day and he said, "Okay, now go to the bank and get them to invest it in something for you with compound interest. They'll be able to show you how you'll have a million by the time you're sixty-five." When I went to the bank, however, I learned they weren't interested in helping me with my hundred-dollar investment. Why? Because it wasn't a moneymaking opportunity for them.

It was a lesson I would learn and relearn over the years. Financial advisors gravitate to people who already have millions of dollars, because managing those millions is how they earn their living. It's not bad or shameful; it's just how it works. The banking system puts a value on people, too. It's nothing personal; it's just the way it works.

My parents always owned their home, and I saw first-hand the opportunities home ownership afforded us over the years. They taught me to start early and make smart decisions. When I learned about what mortgage brokers did—that they helped average people make those same smart decisions—I knew that was what I wanted to do with my life.

I became a mortgage broker in 2004 and immediately realized not many people had mortgage intelligence. At that time, 60 percent of Canadians had a mortgage, but very few people had much clarity about those mortgages. Very few people knew how to use them as a wealth tool, and certainly even fewer people knew about the potential opportunities that could come from aligning themselves with someone who was proactive on their behalf and using every opportunity for their betterment.

I became passionate about helping people use information to their advantage and helping them develop mortgage intelligence, so I quickly became an educator as well. Media outlets started coming to consult me as I grew into being perceived as an expert in the field. People were attracted to me early in my career because they knew my core values were transparency and integrity. I quickly became somebody to watch in the industry, and that media attention developed simultaneously with growth in my business.

I was also a real estate investor. Believe it or not, I was still living with my parents when I purchased my first home! That turned out to be very powerful because later I was able to show people how I'd saved enough to do it so young—and how they could do it, too, if they wanted the same result. I continue to be an active real estate investor as well as a longtime television, radio, and print mortgage expert; I'm often called upon to comment or clarify news in media of all sorts. I developed a huge practice to the point where I'm now consistently receiving a dozen awards a year—from Top Producer to Woman Influencer to Young Gun. I've been awarded the Accredited Mortgage Professional of the Year—the highest award in our industry.

One of the reasons for my success is I'm able to see clarity and opportunities in chaos. I can't control the market, but I can relay information and be clear about it. When you have a passion and desire to be the best that you can be for your community, your industry, your neighbours, and your associates, the rest just follows.

It was the 2008 market shift that put me on the map in an important way. Interest rates fell to half of what they'd been, and everything just froze. Everyone was stunned. Very few people knew what to do. This is a common occurrence when markets are changing, and I was surprised more professionals didn't have clarity around the opportunities inherent in this particular change.

I began to work the numbers. Although penalties were huge for most people who wanted to get out of their mortgages, the numbers made sense for many of them. When we worked the numbers and showed clients what the end result could be if they qualified, on average they cut their payments and amortization in half—even after those significant penalties.

It seemed to me that once you took the fear factor out of it, the recommendations were obvious.

This wasn't even the first time it had happened. In the 1980s, people paid interest rates of 21 percent, and the rates were going down. In the 1990s, the rate was 11 percent, with dips as low as 7 percent. People who had been through this pattern for decades were familiar with the trends. Rates go up and down; that's a part of life. What we have to do as mortgage brokers is understand the math behind the situation and gain clarity for consumers.

In the mortgage world, it's all about getting to the facts. If a client is intimidated about a penalty, it's because they don't understand. It's either worth it to do it, or it's not. There were some cases where it wasn't worth it for clients to make a move, but that doesn't mean that it wouldn't be worth it in the future. It's just about the numbers. I had clients who would have had significant penalties imposed. It didn't make sense at the time to make an immediate change to their mortgages, but it might make sense when they came up for renewal. We diarized it accordingly and contacted them at the right time, and they appreciated our honesty and follow-up.

One of those clients was an officer in the Royal Canadian Mounted Police. I told him we'd keep reviewing his numbers every year until it did make sense, and that's what we did. I reviewed that mortgage twice, in fact, before it actually did start to make sense. Everything finally aligned for him, and we moved forward. The idea is to always place our clients first with a monoline lender so they have the most amount of flexibility to make changes in any market.

This client wasn't initially on board, by the way. What he said is something I hear constantly: "I'm never going to need to make a change again." Experience has taught me this: the people who are the most insistent that nothing is going to change in the next five years are the same people who always have something change in the next five years. That's exactly what happened in this case. Three years later he said, "Hey, I need to make a change."

He was only able to make that change (and save that equity) because of the mortgage we'd put him in. He admitted as much—and since then we've helped his mother and his brother, as he didn't want anyone else he cared about to make the costly mistakes he'd made.

That happens all the time. People always say they're not going to get a divorce, they're not going to want to sell, their job isn't going to change, their health is never going to change, but none of that is true.

None of us can foresee the future, but being as prepared and intelligent as you can will help you navigate it—especially when it comes to mortgages.

WHAT YOU DON'T KNOW

CHAPTER ONE

BUSTING MORTGAGE MARKET MYTHS

There are an amazing number of myths and misconceptions circulating around the mortgage market today. What fuels them and keeps them going is that no one knows they are myths. They are powerful because people believe them to be true.

THE PREAPPROVAL MYTH

A preapproval doesn't mean you're approved. People think that once they get a preapproval, they can go in and make offers with no subject to finance. That's not the case. A preapproval is only a preliminary evaluation of your situation; the lender won't even actually look at your file until the property is in place and the offer has been accepted. Preapprovals are a marketing tactic specifically calculated to get your business.

Imagine if you went to a lender and said, "I'm considering putting an offer in on this particular property; can you give me an approval right now?" If you then looked at another house that you really liked better than the first one, you'd have to go back to the lender and say, "Okay, now I need an approval for this other property." It would be a complete waste of time and resources for any lender.

A preapproval is simply an evaluation of where you are financially. It helps you understand how your job, income, credit, and debt will impact your decision and its outcome. It gives you a general outline that helps you see where you stand. That's all. A preapproval is a rate hold that's done on your behalf; it's when the offer is accepted that the real work gets going, when updated documents are received and property details are reviewed. You might have a preapproval, but the lender might not approve a particular property, or the property might not fall within one of their policies.

A preapproval, in other words, often isn't worth the paper it's written on. Everything can change in a heartbeat, so you can't put too much faith in that document. An expression I use often is that those who have the gold are the ones who make the golden rules, and it applies here: the lenders can always change their minds.

It's not just the lenders who make changes: the Canadian

government has changed mortgage rules in recent years, on average twice a year. Nothing might have changed in your personal circumstances, but the government could step in and make changes that can affect preapprovals.

As I mentioned before, some of this documentation has a short shelf life—thirty days. You may have been pre-approved for a property in January, but you didn't find anything you want, and now it's June. What that means is you'll also need next year's notice of assessments, because by now you've filed your income taxes, and your credit check will need to be updated as well. A statistic that not many people outside the industry know is that only 8 to 12 percent of preapprovals actually go live—that is, make it through the process and move on to become actual approvals.

It's a costly endeavour for lenders to hold an interest rate for you, and so the rate held is often not the rate used. Lenders who allow you to hold interest rates don't generally have the best terms, and the ones with the best terms won't want to hold their money for something that may or may not happen. They're only willing to do it for people who are ready to go.

People often see television or online ads for "instant pre-approval" or "approval in minutes." That's referring to a software app available to every lender, and it essentially gives you some guidelines to help you see approximately where you might stand. The app is helpful in that way—it provides interesting information—but isn't offering anything concrete to the potential borrower.

The takeaway is that all these variables play into the preapproval process. Some mortgage companies even create apps so they don't have to touch files. They don't want to waste their time getting documents and reviewing everything in detail, knowing in advance that only one out of every ten goes live.

That's why we say preapprovals have their place. They can help you determine the factors you'll need to consider when it comes time for the actual approval, and they help you get in the practice of gathering the necessary documentation. Think of it as a worksheet or a trial run. Just understand that, with a 10 to 12 percent closing ratio on preapprovals, lenders can't afford to keep rates competitive and hold that kind of money. It's just not financially feasible.

THE MORTGAGE RATE MYTH

As we saw before, people focus on the mortgage rate and not on the mortgage terms. If you're one of those people, you're not alone! You've been marketed to and brainwashed with the assertion that rate is everything. Rate allows lenders to be competitive with each other and make questions simple. They don't have to work as hard or consider options. They give you the rate and they're done.

You need to understand exactly what the different available interest rates mean; you need to be able to dollarize the amounts. Every five basis points represent about three dollars per hundred thousand. If you're looking at a difference of fifteen basis points—as an example, if someone's offering 2.99 versus 3.14 on a $300,000 mortgage—let's say that's ten dollars a month in difference. Ten times six is sixty. There could be a sixty-dollar difference for that mortgage!

Looking at various mortgage products, if you're taking that 2.99 rate, but you don't know that the mortgage has a sale-only clause, that means that you might not be able to keep that property as a rental. If you were later to divorce, for example, you would then have to sell that property, rather than having the option of one spouse buying out the other. Do you see all the problems that can arise when you're only looking at the interest rate?

You also want to look at the penalty, which might be significantly higher. If you're looking at that same $300,000 mortgage, as an example, your penalty to get out of that mortgage could be 3 to 5 percent of the entire amount.

MORTGAGE PENALTIES COMPARISON

LENDER	AMOUNT	RATE	3 YEARS TO MATURITY	2 YEARS TO MATURITY	DISCOUNT	RATE USED
BANK OF MONTREAL	$250,000	3.39%	$11,175.00	$11,750.00	1.95%	5.34%
ROYAL BANK	$250,000	3.39%	$10,931.06	$10,940.74	1.95%	5.34%
TD CANADA TRUST	$250,000	3.39%	$11,925.00	$11,500.00	1.95%	5.34%
CIBC	$250,000	3.39%	$12,441.85	$11,958.10	1.95%	5.34%
SCOTIABANK	$250,000	3.39%	$10,125.00	$7,250.00	1.95%	5.34%
MCAP	$250,000	3.39%	$3,750.00	$2,118.75	BASED ON CURRENT RATE SPREAD FOR 2, 3 YRS	
FIRST NATIONAL	$250,000	3.39%	$2,817.85	$3,501.68	BASED ON CURRENT RATES FOR 2, 3 YRS	
NATIONAL BANK	$250,000	3.39%	$9,981.25	$11,072.92	BASED ON 2, 3, 4 YR RATE OFF 5.34%	
DOMINION MORTGAGE	$250,000	3.39%	$2,118.75	$2,118.75	BASED ON 3 MTHS INT DIFF WAS LESS	

Why would you choose that lender over one with a slightly higher rate, but whose penalty to get out is 1 percent or less? Wouldn't that be helpful when you have the baby and you need to move up the property ladder? Wouldn't that be helpful when you're cashing in your retirement funds? Wouldn't that be helpful if you have to sell because you're going through a divorce and have that much more money to split? Wouldn't that be helpful if you have outside debt and you need to consolidate? Wouldn't that be helpful if you need money for a down payment for a new place? Wouldn't that be helpful if you have a health problem and need to access your money for private healthcare? Wouldn't that be helpful if interest rates in the market change fifty basis points and you want to take advantage of it by switching to a different lender for a different opportunity?

Why pigeonhole yourself for nothing? People do it because they simply don't know.

Remember that renewing an existing mortgage isn't just porting your mortgage. You have to reapply based on your current qualifications, and the property has to be approved all over again.

THE NO-SUBJECT OFFER MYTH

In competitive housing markets, buyers may feel pressure to move quickly and make seller-friendly offers, often with no subjects such as financing or inspections. It's easy to get caught up in bidding wars for a certain property and give in to internal or external pressure to make offers without subjects, but I'm here to tell you that the no-subject offer is, generally, a bad idea.

As an aside, while I'm mentioning a bidding war, let me be clear that it's absolutely critical for you to have your own real estate agent. You cannot buy from the listing agent. It doesn't matter if you're looking at a brand-new property and you walk into the developer's sales office; no matter what the product is, no matter what the price is, you absolutely need your own representation. Never work directly with the people who are selling the product, because they have a contractual agreement with and obligation to the seller to get them the highest price. Make sure you're taking care of your own needs and have someone who's on your side from the very start.

Clients need to be clear around what their responsibilities are—and what ours are, as well. We will deal with whatever you give us, but if you choose to make a no-subject offer (in the United States, this is called a "no conditions" offer), you are completely responsible for it. We'll do what we can to help you, but if you're going to assume significant risk by not making subjects, that decision is completely your own. You're the only one who can determine how much risk you're willing to assume.

Even if your credit is amazing, your job history stellar, and all your qualifications nearly perfect, the lender still has to approve the property as well, and the problem with no-subject offers is that anything can happen. Even when a file is complete, a lender can always ask for an additional piece of documentation. We've seen files go sideways because the lender has learned something about the property that they weren't aware of upfront.

One example I like telling is that of an individual who wanted to make a no-subject offer, planning on retiring after the mortgage got approved. He thought everything was perfect. Then the HR director from the borrower's company called the lender and let them know that even though the employee/borrower had been fully employed at the time of the approval, he'd retired in the two weeks since. The lender withdrew the approval—and the borrower had no contingency plans. Fortunately, he was a teacher and still receiving a pension, so was able to make alternate financial plans; but that won't be true for everyone. All kinds of things can happen. We helped the client, of course, but there was a lot of unnecessary stress in the process.

There are things that happen outside of our control, outside of your control, outside of anyone's control. The only thing you can control is your impulse to be competitive in an extremely competitive market. All we can do, in turn, is advise you as to your options.

Another consideration is that there's no such thing as a preapproval on a no-subject offer. You only have one chance to get it right. If the lender you've selected pulls out for any reason—the lender isn't happy about something, the appraisal doesn't agree with the price, or any of a myriad of other possibilities—then you'll need to scramble to find alternate financing, often at a higher rate and via a more restrictive product. We would probably advise you not to do it. We'll help you figure out how to deal with it, but the bottom line is that it's never the best option.

Lenders are often a little lackadaisical about the process as well, and many lenders are, in fact, willing to take risks. They'll agree with you that the no-subject offer will work out perfectly well. Just remember that the person telling you everything's going to be okay is not the person giving you the money. They're going to try and get approval to get you the money, and a lot of the time it works—but sometimes it doesn't. We get calls when it doesn't: "Our bank said everything was fine and then it wasn't, so now we're coming to you."

Some providers like to tell people what they want to hear. I won't say that delivering bad or unpopular news is pleasant; of course it isn't. But that's the job. If you want everyone to like you, you sell ice cream for a living; you don't become a mortgage professional. Doing the right thing for a client is not the same as always making that client happy!

The truth is that most people want someone to tell them they're okay. "You didn't say I couldn't eat a McDonald's super-sized meal and still lower my blood pressure!" Everyone regresses slightly under stress, and moving is one of the biggest stressors out there—right on the same level as death and divorce.

We absolutely understand the stress you're under, and we understand the human tendency to want to share the anxiety and, if necessary, the blame. We understand it, but we're not going to take part in it.

The only way to be able to have a no-subject offer and not expect any stress is to have a 100 percent down payment. That's your solution. It's the only way you can be sure—at least where the financing is concerned. There are just too many factors that can come into play, too many things that can happen that you can't anticipate. Let's say you have an inspection done and there's a problem, so you decrease the offer. The lender wants to know why your price has decreased, and they can even turn down their offer or lend you less now.

You also might get a mortgage that is not for the terms you wanted, or you find out that it's limited to a certain amount. Say the appraisal comes in, but it's disappointing. Just because someone's willing to pay a certain amount for a house doesn't mean the banks are willing to lend that much. Bank appraisers are always on the conservative side.

The economic life remaining on the house can also come into play. You might look at a house and think, *Oh, my goodness, how can you say it's only got an economic life of twenty years left? I could easily see myself living here for fifty years.* It's not about you. The appraiser can reduce the amount, or the amortization, and ultimately that's going to cause you even more stress as you try to decide whether you want to proceed or not.

You might decide to go to a lender that has different terms. Or you might decide to go with one that's more lenient but with poorer terms, and you might decide it's all worth it if it gets you the property you want. There might be a discrepancy between you and the property, another situation that can change the terms of your mortgage. You might be considered an A-level client but you're looking at a B-level property, according to that lender's property criteria. The best rates and the best terms are reserved for the best credit applicants and the most prime properties.

There are a hundred things that can go wrong once the lender starts scrutinizing the property. The piping in a building might not be the piping they agreed to. There's a zoning mix of commercial and residential properties and they don't like it. They might not agree with the engineer's report, or they might not agree with what route the strata took to handle an issue. They might not be willing to do it because of a lawsuit happening on the strata. There could be all kinds of reasons things don't go as planned, as hoped for, or as anticipated. That's the bad news. The good news is we've got a tremendous amount of experience dealing with these types of scenarios and can help guide you through.

There will always be the mortgage equivalent of turbulence. One of our clients, an airline pilot, told us, "We get blamed for turbulence all the time! Any pilot will keep the ride as smooth as possible, but weather does change and reports can be wrong. We do our best to avoid it, but we can't control the skies." The truth is, sometimes turbulence happens. What matters is how you deal with it. Any good mortgage professional will navigate you safely through any turbulence that arises in your mortgage application.

All in all, the no-subject offer isn't one we recommend. We can help if it's the route you choose to take, but we'll also show you all the options from which you can choose.

THINK DIFFERENTLY

To move up the property ladder, you need a new mindset.

Too many people approach mortgages with a transactional mindset. You apply for your mortgage; you get your mortgage; good-bye.

That's not the way we see it working. We see ourselves in a long-term relationship with our clients. If you think of mortgages in transactional terms, they're just a tool to get you into the house you want. If you think of mortgages in relational terms, then they become part of an overall financial strategy.

I am truly excited about saving people money. I'm excited about meeting new people and knowing that I'm going to have such a positive impact on their lives. I know what an important decision acquiring a mortgage is, and how much it's going to change people's lives going forward, and that's why I'm passionate about all of this: about saving money and about educating consumers. They go hand in hand.

Your mortgage will play the most significant role in your wealth-acquisition planning. For that to happen, you have to maintain the most equity and be able to modify the mortgage based on your life needs. Those modifications are critical to your future success.

Having the best mortgage helps you through all the things life can throw at you. Obviously, there are myriad things you can't control—a major health issue, an accident, divorce, and death. You can't control the real estate market or the interest rate market. You can't control what happens around you globally with resources and import and export and the bond market—in fact, the list of what you can't control goes on and on.

What you can control is getting the best possible mortgage product. If you have a mortgage product with the lowest exit strategy because you've been positioned to be able to do that, then you're able to always keep the most equity in your pocket and be in the most control possible of your personal circumstances.

Times have changed, they're still changing, and they will always change. The markets, the rates, your life, everything. Your mortgage could be costing you thousands just when you need the money the most, unless you have a relationship with a broker who has your best interests in mind.

Who is that broker? Essentially, it's someone who is in it for the long haul, who is looking for ongoing relationships with their clients. Assembling the right team—a team that is proactive and shows accountability and adaptability—is critical.

Finding the right team starts with understanding, yet

again, that a mortgage is not about the interest rate you get. The way you determine the value of your mortgage is in exactly what you pay and the modifications of the terms. That's the beginning. Moving forward, that can only happen if you're managing it proactively.

A good team does what mine does: keeps you abreast of all the changes happening in the marketplace so you understand them and can reach out if you want to consult about them.

A good team looks at every single mortgage, every single year. They reach out to you and see if anything has changed in your life stage, your employment, or any other circumstances to ensure they're always optimizing the market to the best of their ability. They're also reviewing the interest rate and comparing it to what's out there today to get in front of any changes. Unlike the majority of brokers, and all of the banks, they're not reactive. They're monitoring everything and helping you make the best decisions possible for your financial well-being.

This reminds me of a young couple we helped. They worked in a car dealership; the woman worked at the front desk and her boyfriend was a mechanic. They wanted to buy a home, and I knew about a new mortgage product that had just come out and gave the option of no money down provided they had good credit. We had to work with them to show them how to rehab their credit so they could take advantage of the product. When they got that product, they stayed in their home and built a lot of equity, and we continued to follow their lives.

They got married and had two children. When the first term was up on their mortgage, we helped them renew it with a different lender, because the first lender didn't offer what was the best scenario for them. We found a lender that allowed them to consolidate some outside debt and save money so they could qualify to move up the property ladder. A few years later, they moved into another house; they'd paid their mortgage down significantly without payment shock because we'd already trained them for that when they were in their first home.

This case study worked because we kept them updated with the products and offers that were out there, and we proactively managed their mortgage so they were able to take advantage of the changing situations presented to them. We researched their options, we considered when they wanted to sell and move up the property ladder, we knew that their income had to be in a particular place, and we worked with them to get there. Everything was done methodically and strategically to ensure their success. That wouldn't have happened if they had been out on their own trying to figure out the market, or even if we reactively touched base just once in a while. It's our methodical approach to always seeing what's best for each one of our clients that helps them acquire mortgage intelligence.

CHANGE YOUR APPROACH

Too many people get stuck asking the wrong questions. Why do you need these documents? Why shouldn't I get that kind of mortgage? Why can't I give you something else instead? Why do you have to know about my plans for next year? What is the mortgage rate?

People get stuck because they approach mortgages differently than they approach anything else in their lives. No one would ask a doctor for a diagnosis and treatment plan before the doctor finished evaluating the patient's condition. That would be laughable. Why should mortgages be any different? Why shouldn't we have all the facts in hand so we can offer you a treatment plan with the best long-term prognosis?

Sometimes this is just because most people don't know the right questions to ask. Some people think they have a lot going for them in terms of success—financial and otherwise—and they assume they'll qualify for any mortgage they want.

It also doesn't mean they'll be able to shop sensibly. As I'm writing this, there is one lender who appears to be offering the best variable rate mortgage. Sounds great, right? Wrong: what they're not advertising is that they have a higher prime rate than every other lender in the country.

It's not the lender's job to tell you what is different about their offering. It's up to you as a borrower to align yourself with people who can take the time to educate you and give you the transparency you need to make sound decisions. You would think it's common sense that you deserve transparency with your finances, but it's not. It's your responsibility to find and work with people who can give you that. It's no one's responsibility to give you everything on a silver platter; it's your responsibility to ensure you've asked the right questions, you've aligned yourself with the right people, and you've got the checks and balances in place to fully optimize everything in your life—finances or otherwise.

Perhaps you understand about rates but are confused about policies. Take prepayment privileges as an example. Every single lender has different ones, with tricky wording and vastly different outcomes. Lenders may offer a 10 percent prepayment policy. Do you know whether that's a good deal or not? (Hint: it isn't.) But it gets worse: even if you like that percentage, what you don't know is that it's only good for one day, your mortgage anniversary date. That would be good to know, right?

Lenders aren't going to tell you these things. You have to

ask, and most people don't know what to ask about or how to ask it. One of the most common costly mistakes I see is a lender increasing a client's payments without telling them, since the increase is considered a "privilege." The client can't return to reducing those payments unless they spend the money it takes to break the mortgage.

In essence, if you can't prepay properly, you can be faced with future payment shock, higher costs down the road (e.g., using unsecured debt to pay for things), or a penalty you'd need to pay to get a better mortgage. All of which increases your cost of borrowing.

These are all reasons why we consistently and collaboratively assist our clients, helping with prepayments when lenders allow them and making sure the clients have clarity on the whole picture. Each lender has their place, and people make decisions based on their mortgage understanding.

The real conclusion here is that you can't do better until you know better, and cracking the mortgage code is paramount for your success. We have it, and we want you to have it, too. We want you to ask the right questions. We want to offer you full transparency. We want to work as a team so you can accomplish your goals. You won't be able to do any of those things until you understand what it is that you're doing wrong. You won't be able to do any of those things until you can grasp the financial questions you should be asking yourself at different points in your life.

The mortgage market is tricky to navigate. We know how to help you get from Point A to Point R or Point S or wherever it is you see yourself in ten, twenty, thirty years. We'll offer you our knowledge, our years of experience, our financial acumen, and a commitment to be with you throughout all the changes that will happen in your life.

We'll begin by making sure you understand the concept of debt.

CHAPTER TWO

ALL DEBT IS DEBT

Owning a home is about understanding how to use it as a wealth-building tool. If you restructure your debt, it frees up cash flow to help you move quickly up the property ladder. In spite of this relatively straightforward action plan, many people approach mortgage management in all the wrong ways.

CONSOLIDATE AND CONQUER

A common way of thinking is, "I need to pay my mortgage off as fast as possible." But when people think that way, they're usually not looking at the outside, higher-rate debt they're carrying. Unless you're in line for a huge bonus at work (unlikely for most Canadians), or proceeds are rolling in from the sale of personal assets, or you're the lucky recipient of an inheritance, the likelihood of paying off your outside debt is next to nil. And that debt cripples your opportunities to help with your biggest debt—your mortgage.

Most people recommend against adding credit card debt, a car loan, or a student loan to your mortgage, but it's actually the best thing you can do. It is most beneficial for you to improve your cash flow, save money every month, and stop the cycle of debt to improve your credit score. This in turn improves your ability to move up the property ladder if you so choose or start buying revenue-generating investments as soon as possible. Every day you delay, you're throwing money out the window.

Consider the example of Deena, a city councillor with two credit card balances and a line of credit. We consolidated that debt into her mortgage and it saved her $1,600 a month.

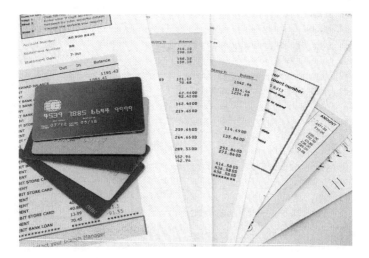

The sooner you can take care of your debt, the sooner you can get equity working for you. People often think they're in great shape simply because they have paid down their mortgage. That doesn't amount to much if you still have a bundle of debt elsewhere.

Once you've eliminated outside debt, you can save for retirement, buy dividend-paying investments, put money aside for emergencies, or help your family. For example, a lot of parents would rather help their children while the parents are still in good health, rather than after they pass on. Many people would like to start a business or do something special for themselves. If you have crippling outside debt, however, there's no way to do any of those things.

Traditional living expenses are another area of concern. If you don't have six months of living expenses available in a bank account, you are a vulnerable target in a financial crisis. When we redid Deena's mortgage, it freed up a substantial amount of money for other expenses. That was just one example. It doesn't mean everyone can do that. Some people will save more and some will save less, but saving at all opens up so many opportunities. I did a mortgage for a newspaper editor and he said, "I don't have a pension, but now I'll be able to save for my retirement and I can buy that house by the lake, or maybe a condo I can rent out. Then I can sell my house and downsize into the condo."

It very quickly becomes a family affair. Once we help one person in a family, we end up helping their children or aunts and uncles or grandparents. When they learn what we can do for them and the difference in service that's available, they quickly become keen on this process. And who wouldn't?

On the other hand, banks make the most money on credit cards and lines of credit, so they sell those all day long. There's a reason why the qualification process for a credit card or line of credit is so simple; it's just a matter of a few clicks online or making a phone call. They don't verify anything because credit balances generate a great deal of money. Every day that you continue to pay on that balance instead of getting your money working for you (in your mortgage, for example), the better it is for the bank.

Credit checks and scores are formidable obstacles as well. Every time you do a credit check, it takes five points off your score. Carrying outside debt higher than 20 percent below the balance hurts your credit score. Carrying less than two or three active credit scenarios hurts your credit score. You want to aim for the best possible credit score, because that will result in the best product for you—and the best lender choices. A lower-than-average credit score means you will likely need to take a mortgage option that could be more expensive and will entail more work getting a better mortgage when your credit improves.

Borrowers should always remember to avoid checking their credit scores when mortgage shopping, because points are taken off every time you check. But when we use your application to shop out the lenders, we use only the one application, and lenders will accept it from us. Whereas if you go in unaware to a new lender with your information already on hand, it's easy for the lender to pull a score and not even let you know they're doing it. This is a burden everyone can do without!

THE MIDDLE-CLASS DEBT BURDEN

Six out of ten Canadians (and seven out of ten Americans) live pay cheque to pay cheque with wages that are largely stagnant. It's nearly impossible for people to find more time in the day to even get a second job. Our routine is common: get up, get the kids ready for school, take them to school, work all day, race to activities and then home for dinner, crash to sleep, and repeat the next day. It's a constant battle just to keep going, and that's why I'm so passionate about helping people get ahead by intelligently using what they already have to their advantage.

There are myriad misconceptions around financial lenders, and we're constantly bombarded with marketing. Available options are either complicated or completely hidden unless you can find someone unbiased and transparent who can find a way to save $1,600 a month.

When we meet clients for the first time, all sorts of things happen when they realize they've been losing money for years. Bad financial news can be a bitter pill to swallow and typically people become excited, embarrassed, defensive, even angry at the system and at everyone involved. Here's the bottom line: you're responsible for aligning yourself with the right person at the right time, and if in the past you didn't, you can fix that now.

No one has the energy to sift through financial clutter. Everyone's tired. I've never heard anyone say, "I have so much energy and time to spare!" That just isn't reality. Time is fleeting, with new demands constantly adding to already busy lives. Once you get good at something, there's someone who will want you to get better. Once you meet a target at work, your boss is already giving you more to do. It never seems to end.

My company recognizes that. We empathize with the struggles and internal scenarios people face every day. A couple might be juggling their finances and making a mess of it, each one assuming the other is in control. There are all sorts of scenarios that happen out there in the real world, reasons why people's finances got to the state they're in. We don't judge anyone. We're not here to do anything but take the current scenario and make it the best it can be. If we can't do that, we'll explain why—and what you can do right now to improve your situation. Then we'll talk again to develop a workable strategy.

None of this is your fault. Times have changed. In the not-too-distant past, you might have spent your career with a single company, and you could count on receiving a solid retirement package. That is a rarity today. Now, people need to create their own retirement plans. But if you're throwing away tens of thousands of dollars in unnecessary interest on credit cards when you could have consolidated that into your mortgage and saved money every month to put toward your retirement, you feel like kicking yourself.

And then add to those problems external ones. Whenever third parties review and report your credit, there's potential for fraud. The financial scandal in 2017 caused havoc with people's credit scores. Unfortunately, customers are the ones saddled with the burden of mistakes until whatever the mess is gets fixed.

In other situations, it is usually what people don't tell you that costs you. There are companies that spend millions of dollars on marketing with promises about cutting your debt, but don't tell you how they plan to do that. There are a lot of companies calling themselves "credit counsellors" or "trustees," but their focus is making money for themselves, not for you.

Some of these companies negotiate on behalf of credit card companies to help with your particular situation, and they charge a fee to do it. But people don't realize how these negotiations might impact their credit, and they especially don't know there are alternatives. Traditional lender negotiation may well be your best option. When that's the case, my company will direct you down that path because we've reviewed your situation and it's the right thing to do. That's part of the integrity of who we are and how we've built our business.

When something comes up and people want things quickly, many companies prey on consumers' emotions. They'll say, "Hey, get your home equity working for you!" What they won't say is it will cost an array of fees eating into your equity. You might have done better somewhere else—but how were you to know? People sometimes have to use those companies due to specific circumstances in their lives at a given time, but it should only be a last resort. If you work with a competent mortgage planner, you'll understand why you're there and what you can expect. If you approach those companies on your own, you're asking to be sold a product that may or may not be okay for you. Takeaway tip? Don't fall for client-direct advertising.

If any of those options are good for you, we will recommend them to you.

In some instances, when we work collaboratively with

a client on a project and the credit score isn't where we want it to be, we'll ask the client to go and check their own credit score and send it to us instead of us doing it. We don't want to take points off their score. We tell them. We might not be able to help them at that moment, but we'll make a plan to move forward in three months, for example, and in the meantime we'll tell the client some concrete steps they can take.

Again, it's collaborative. We never send people away and say, "Don't come to us." Everything we do is collaborative, transparent, and unbiased. We are here to do the best thing for you, period.

Many people reading this book are likely by now wondering, "Do I have the best mortgage? Could it be better? What can I do about it?" The answer is easy: just email us. Grab your phone or other handy device and send a note that says, "Hey, can you let me know how I can get my mortgage reviewed?" Simple. Once you've taken that step, we'll take care of the rest. We'll contact you briefly, ask a few questions, request some information, and give you a straight answer.

I'm confident when you are finished reading this book, you'll get on the phone. Just send the email while you're reading this. Don't let anything time-bandit you.

That's how it all starts. A lot of people hear my radio show on CKNW. The show has been running for years; it's the longest-running mortgage show in Canada. I hear comments like, "I was cleaning my bathroom when I heard you talking about how you helped someone. As soon as I finished, I sent you an email." Shift workers—like nurses and police officers—offer comments such as, "I was patrolling and I heard your show," or "I was driving home from my afternoon shift and I heard you talking about this, so I thought I'd better get in touch with you."

It's always interesting to me to hear where people are when they hear someone or about something that changes their life.

NOT ALL DEBT IS BAD DEBT

Debt is a part of life. The secret is in managing it and not letting it grow out of control. It's natural to compare yourself to other people and set yourself up with false expectations, thinking that you should be in a certain place at a certain time in your life. But you need to do it when it's right for you.

Having a home, for example, does mean taking on some debt in the form of a mortgage, but it also offers the opportunity to get ahead financially. If you don't own a home, you can't consolidate your debt and get your money working for you in different ways. But don't fault yourself if your circumstances don't allow it yet. We're here to help you regardless of your life stage, regardless of what life has thrown at you.

We can even act as your financial concierge, working directly with your accountant and other parties to get things done. We can often make things happen more quickly than you could manage on your own, and with a lot less stress. If there is something we can suggest to improve your financial well-being, we'll review the options and position you accordingly. We may select a better time to review based on your financials and get answers in advance for questions we anticipate, to ensure the smoothest process possible. Getting things in piecemeal—or, worse, giving it to a lender in piecemeal—doesn't position the client in the best light.

This is part of why we're so successful. Our lenders count on us to know our job and submit things properly and in perfect order. When they have a rate special, they're going to offer it to someone who makes their job easier and completes everything within the right process and following the rules.

We're all constantly bombarded with marketing, and it's possible to be influenced so much by it that you become convinced you want something when it's not what you actually need. We just completed a mortgage for a Vancouver lawyer who was certain she wanted a particular product. When we told her why she shouldn't go in that direction, she appreciated that we knew the best product for her based on her goals. She also appreciated we're not just order-takers, and realized other lenders simply offer what pleases clients without revealing all the available options. She had set herself up for what was potentially a costly mistake, but she also knew we wouldn't let her do anything that went against her best interests. We'd done mortgages for many of her coworkers and she knew we would get the best for her.

In other situations, people simply do not have funds needed to make ends meet, resorting to credit cards to pay bills. This reflects on our discussion of debt consolidation. We can help you stop the cycle of debt and establish monthly savings to provide a financial cushion. We also look to see if we can take out extra money to give you six months' padding so you won't be in that scenario again.

MOVING UP THE PROPERTY LADDER

Let's look at an example of a hard-working couple in Vancouver, an engineer and a nurse, who were hoping to move into their dream home. Both were high-income earners with an existing mortgage up for renewal in a year and a half. They hadn't planned on doing anything until then, but they thought they'd start looking around at their options.

We immediately identified financial pain points. It wasn't monthly payments that were holding them back, or that they had any glaring financial burden; what they didn't know was they would never be able to qualify for a new home based on their current debt load.

When they stopped to think about it, they had upgraded their half-duplex home quite a lot over the few years they'd lived there, including purchasing new furniture. They had a vehicle break down, resulting in a large repair bill. The husband returned to school to get his master's degree and had to pay for it with credit. These things accumulated into a relatively significant debt load, but because they were high-income earners, it didn't impact their day-to-day lives or cause noticeable financial stress. However, the debt was enough of an obstacle to block them from moving up the property ladder.

The most effective strategy to help them qualify for more was to consolidate their debts, providing a savings of more than $1,400 a month. That savings allowed their cash flow to be deployed in the best possible manner and they avoided paying unnecessary interest.

Debt can add up even with a modest lifestyle. Life goes

by quickly and it's easy to not think about money issues, especially if you can afford your payments. In this couple's scenario, they didn't view it as a negative until they realized they wouldn't qualify to move up the property ladder.

They thought it would be a couple of years until they made that leap, but as a result of getting everything in order, moving things along in a more efficient manner, and with beneficial timing in the market, they were able to move into their dream home a lot sooner.

CHAPTER THREE

WHAT THE BANKS WON'T TELL YOU

Banks keep secrets.

They're not evildoers, not even close; but as I mentioned earlier, banks make decisions in their own best interests. And while banks and related lenders also have responsibilities to their clients, borrowers must carefully consider a lender's history in order to understand whom they're aligning themselves with.

The biggest mistake that borrowers don't even know they're making when they walk into a bank looking for a mortgage is believing the bank is there to do what's best for them. That's simply not the case. A bank's goal is to do what's best for its shareholders. The bank will absolutely offer you the best mortgage product it can but isn't going to tell you how that product compares to what other lenders are offering. No one at the bank is ever going to tell you that sometimes the bank costs consumers money rather than helping them save.

This doesn't mean that what the bank is offering isn't your absolute best option. It absolutely could be. But what it means is that you don't have choices, and so you don't know what your best option is.

A lender's goal is to make money for their institution. If you go directly to them, you won't be getting unbiased information. They won't tell you, for example, if they have a special "quick closing rate" prior to completion, because they've already signed you at the higher rate. If they can sell high-ratio insurance instead of doing a top-up, they will, because it double insures them. If they have the opportunity to tack on additional charges, they generally will.

It is something of a grey area, but a lot of lenders do package selling, where they explain that in order to get this offer, you need to bring x amount of money over to us. But they don't make any guarantee to manage that money in a beneficial manner. Many lenders will also often require or strongly suggest in order to compensate for the "favour they did you" the purchase of a specific insurance in order to be part of an offer.

How can you sort through all this? If you go to a qualified and proactive mortgage broker, you'll be getting straight information without any bias. You'll be able to see clearly which option is best for you, because you'll be offered several—along with sound advice as to which to select.

Many lenders will say a mortgage is portable, which means you can move it with you when you sell your home and move to a new one. (This is only true in the Canadian market; in the United States, mortgages are tied to one property only.) While mortgages are generally tied to the property in question, even in Canada, when you have a portable mortgage, you and your lender are agreeing to sign it over to a new property. Some mortgages are portable; some aren't. Portability doesn't mean a lot, because you'll still have to re-qualify, but framing and selling a mortgage as portable sounds good, doesn't it? I go back to the example of a woman who was stuck with her mortgage for four additional years because she wasn't told the mortgage had a specific term. She couldn't refinance her mortgage unless she sold her home.

This also reminds me of another client, a private banker who worked for one of the major lenders, who approached me and said, "I have my mortgage with a credit union right now, and they won't allow me to port my high-ratio insurance on my purchase." The client had sold her home and was looking to move her family into a new construction development.

The first thing we do when a client upgrades in size from one house to another is look to see if we can save them money on the high-ratio purchase by using that same insurance and just topping up for the new amount. In this case, I was able to save this woman and her family $10,000.

Again, if banks have the opportunity to recharge a fee, they probably will. Every lender has different policies regarding what they will or will not allow. Some will mirror the policies of the insurer, and others will not.

I've been a member of the board of advisors for large Canadian insurers. Because of the volume of business that I do, I generally have the opportunity to sit one-on-one with risk managers, product development managers, and business development managers, and discuss different ins and outs of a product to ensure we've aligned ourselves with a lender that best reflects the benefits of the product.

As an example, my client's initial mortgage holder was a credit union that didn't mirror the policies of the insurer. It was the insurer's, not the bank's, policy that the client could have up to six months to port the insurance premium.

Customers need to understand that financial institutions

have certain policies, and although they might want to give you the world, they can't change the terms associated with their mortgages. We aren't bound by any one lender's policies. I always tell my clients we're here to do the best for them. And if that means they need to stick with a specific lender, that's fine. I go back to the reason why we're here: we are in this business because we believe in transparency and honesty when it comes to your finances.

The private banker who came to me for assistance didn't do her mortgage with her own bank. That's pretty meaningful and is extremely common. I had another private banker from an area financial institution, someone with a salary on the high side of $600,000 a year. Their number-one job is to recruit high net worth individuals—doctors, lawyers, and corporations—to have their deposits on hand. It's all about profit. When banks have your money on deposit, they lend it out at about eight times its worth. Every single dollar is worth about eight dollars to the bank.

(You have to be wary of titles: the "private banker" might be a title to make you feel special, but you can't trust that this is actually someone who will be more helpful to you. Titles feed egos, so look at titles and ask yourself what really is behind them!)

In British Columbia, it's becoming more and more common for people to have large mortgages on residential properties, anywhere between $800,000 and $3 million in certain areas, while Canada-wide the average is $350,000. Every lending institution has different sliding scales on how much mortgage they'll lend before scaling back. Sometimes, high-end clients don't get the best deals when working directly with lenders, because the lenders know they're less likely to shop around due to the complexity of their finances and the title of the person working on their file. That's just another reason to use an independent mortgage professional!

We continually see high-income earners and people working in the business come to my company for their mortgage needs. We do want clients with good credit, with high income, people we can help see how the system hasn't benefitted them and how we can make a difference. The wealthiest and smartest people look to align themselves with others who know the system to get the most out of it.

I'm reminded of another private banker who was buying a home for five million dollars in North Vancouver. His bank's interest rate was high and came with fixed terms and policies. Remember, he did mortgages and business with the elite top 1 percent in the country, but he was better off not going through his own institution! He came to us instead.

Of course, different banks have different policies at different times, and everything in this business ebbs and flows. At one time, the bank where he works might have offered the best mortgage, but in that specific snapshot in time, it didn't. We got him a better rate, better terms, and a higher mortgage. Lenders' jobs are to sell these things, but they know when they want the best, they still come to a mortgage professional.

It's difficult to understand the psychology of why people would go to a lender on their own, when their lender only has one box with just a few products in it. You either fit or you don't, and if you don't know to ask, you'll never know what is and isn't in that box because these are things that are just not discussed. And how would you ever know to ask?

I'm not trying to paint banks in a bad light. In fact, I'm grateful to them. Many people are unaware that banks provide lenders with funds and with excellent terms. Major banks are the biggest investors in monoline companies because these companies only lend mortgages, so they can keep their costs down and offer you preferential rates, products, and services. And if a bank's product is the best option for you, we will recommend it. We just have more options.

All this just reinforces that a great mortgage broker is your best bet for ensuring your financial future.

THE INTEREST RATE DIFFERENTIAL FACTOR

The interest rate differential is in the housing market to describe the difference between the interest rate and a bank's posted rate on the prepayment date for mortgages.

It's next to impossible to intelligently shop for a mortgage because the wording in any lender's commitment is like trying to read an alien language. People often say, "Well, I have the mortgage commitment here from my bank, and I have the mortgage commitment from you, and they say the same thing."

Just because the documents say the same thing doesn't mean they have the same meaning. They're from two different lenders. Major retail banks have posted rates, and the discount equates to the rate customers actually pay. Banks frame the program to make it seem like you're getting a great deal.

A bank might say, "Well, we gave you 2 percent off our posted rate," and you think you got an amazing deal with that 2 percent off. But lenders that deal only with mortgage brokers only have fully discounted rates to begin with, so, congratulations: you've essentially received a 0 percent discount!

Here's the kicker: that "2 percent discount" is used against you when you make a modification down the road. It can cost you up to $15,000 to get out of a $300,000 mortgage. With a monoline lender, it will cost a maximum of $4,500.

In their defence, major banks are our partners and have excellent products based on your life stage. They serve a purpose, depending on your qualifications, the property, and the timing of your purchase. Monoline lenders typically want prime properties or plum clients with a 700-plus credit score. If you can qualify for a monoline mortgage based on market fitness, your credit, income, and investment strategy, then you'll be better off. It's the first place we look, for obvious reasons; it's just that not everybody fits there. Wherever you fit is where you'll get the best deal.

If a client is closing in on retirement, for example, they might consider different tax strategies.

I have a client who's a pipefitter. Dan's in a monoline mortgage, but I need to get him out of it because I need exceptions on the ratio for his income beyond what that lender will do. He is making a commercial purchase, but he no longer qualifies with a monoline lender; I have to pull out more money than his current lender will allow. In this case, I have to put my client with a major bank that will offer favourable opportunities and allow him to reach his goals. The upside, however, is significant because of the leverage it will offer my client for building his wealth.

There's always a time and a place for banks, but you have to go to an independent mortgage professional to learn about what your best options might be. I don't represent only one institution. My income isn't dependent on having to sell x number of financial packages.

That's a significant difference between independent mortgage brokers and banks. Banks have specific targets. They have a set number of people they want to sell to on a variable, a specific number to sell on a fixed, and a target number of credit cards and lines of credit. That's how they're structured. We do things completely differently. We look at the best solution for the borrower considering their lifestyle, income, credit, timing in the market, and everything they are looking to do. We get compensated regardless of where we place the mortgage.

As consumers get more familiar and smarter with finances, the banks will stay one step ahead and reword or rephrase things. For example, customers focus on the interest rate, but they don't know enough about terms, and don't put terms as the number one priority. Banks will offer an "easy" variable rate mortgage. But that variable rate mortgage could easily have a penalty associated with it that could be equal to an interest rate differential or percentage of the mortgage as well. "Low rate advantage mortgages" (also called "smart" mortgages) are all about marketing: the name means nothing. Unless you have a complete understanding of what those terms mean by way of an independent professional, you're guaranteed that at some point you'll be paying more than you have to.

Lenders can play games with interest rates. I always look at the lender's history. Who's the first to raise their interest rates? Who's the last? Who has demonstrated new territory for changing policies, or aligns themselves with insurer policies? You might not think that's important but changing rates can have a tremendous impact on your finances.

For the last thirty years, every lender has decided to decrease, raise, or keep the same rates in conjunction with the prime rate as it moves with Bank of Canada rate announcements. One bank decided to buck the trend, choosing to offer a higher prime rate than everybody else and not move its rates in conjunction with the Bank of Canada.

That one bank is consistent for being the first to raise its rates, the last to decrease its rates, and—for lack of better words—for finding ways to take money out of its borrowers' pockets. Strategically, it was a smart move from the bank's point of view, because of how they control their payments. They don't change your principal and interest payment amounts. What changes is only the distribution of principal and interest. They looked at their portfolio, and they saw an instant way to make profit without a huge backlash, because consumers wouldn't be impacted.

Most consumers don't notice immediately that there's been a change; they really only notice over time when their amortization goes up. That can also happen when there's a trigger clause; it's extremely unusual, but lenders are changing all the time, so it's essential to stay on top of changes.

HOW CAN I KEEP UP?

How can customers keep up with all of this? Banks generally only send you letters when their rates go up. It's unusual to see a bank say, "Hey, we've just reduced our rates. Come and take advantage of it." They only do promotions for "new clients." So, as a consumer, how do you know their history? If you're not in the mortgage market, or if you haven't had a mortgage with them before, how would you know? What they publish doesn't necessarily mean it's legit.

You need to find someone with experience dealing with

these types of lenders. In my experience, when I deal with monoline lenders, they allow me to help my clients lock in if they've selected a variable rate. The banks don't do that for a reason. If they did, the process would move quickly and they would lose money. If they can delay the process, that increases their profit.

What I'm trying to articulate is that you have a choice, a choice average consumers won't understand—and the bank won't help you understand.

Why would they? A bank representative's income is generated from promoting that brand and being a brand ambassador. They're not obligated to tell you anything that doesn't increase the bank's profit. Different lenders may adopt different policies, but if you look at the history you can usually predict what to expect from them in the future.

From my end, I can't control anything. I can't control what may or may not happen. All I can do is use my experience to share how we can help our customers. What lenders are not telling you is costing you money. Lenders are motivated by profit; I'm motivated to earn loyalty by giving clients a good current experience and educating them at the same time.

Banks provide needed resources, and the last thing I want

to do is cast them in a negative light. In fact, even if you work with a monoline lender, that lender is essentially using money from investors, which brings us back to the banks. Banks are the source of most mortgage funding. We need them. But what you need is someone to act on your behalf and present you to the best possible fit.

Let's talk about running mortgage accounts. Lenders don't tell you how they register their mortgages, so they might sell you a product for a much higher amount than the actual value. Let me give you an example. If you get a mortgage with a particular bank or credit union for $500,000, they can register it at $1.5 million. In effect, they squat on your property and sell it as a feature, saying you could potentially access that money in the future. What they don't tell you is you have to re-qualify to get it. They also won't tell you that it prevents anyone else from registering behind them.

Whereas currently, if you have a mortgage with a monoline lender, in most cases the lender only registers the property for the mortgage they have on hand. If you have a property worth $1 million, and they have a mortgage of $300,000, they only register it as a single charge at $300,000. This doesn't become a big deal until your mortgage is up for renewal. As an example, as of this writing there are certain lenders that will pay for your legal fees to transfer the mortgage over. If it's registered as a running account, however, they often can't do that, and you might end up paying new legal fees for the transfer.

Whichever is the best solution, we'll find it for you.

ALL IN A NAME

Again, it's how the conversation is framed. Lenders will portray a product as a great option for you that offers certain advantages, but what they won't disclose is you're limiting your options upon the renewal of your mortgage as well. Remember, it's always what they're not saying that's important to listen to. If you hear, "Hey, it's great; we might have this option for you," keep in mind it means you can't get a line of credit somewhere else, because now someone has to register a second or third mortgage.

Sometimes lenders will say, "Oh, we can't register a line of credit behind this lender."

Yes, they can.

As long as it's not a running account, they can register. They frame the pitch with the perks of running a mortgage through their facility, but they don't explain the disadvantages. And you can't blame them: it's not their responsibility to hold your hand. That responsibility rests with an independent mortgage professional who will make sure to answer even the questions you don't know to ask. As a borrower, it's prudent to confirm you understand.

To be fair, I do have to say that people forget a lot of what goes on during the process. We've had people with variable rate mortgages that have remained the same or decreased for years, and then as soon as rates go up, they say, "I didn't want a variable; I wanted a fixed." The opposite scenario is also common, when rates decrease and customers clamour for a variable rate.

You'll minimize both confusion and potential financial stress if you go to a mortgage professional. Both mortgage approval examples read that to get out of the mortgage, it's either the IRD or the three-month interest. One has posted rates; one does not. What does that mean? You have a 2 percent discount off one, and a 0 percent discount off the other. Who knows which is the best? In terms of framing the conversation and marketing, people think 2 percent off is better than 0 percent off.

LENDERS' RESPONSIBILITIES

As much as consumers try to be aware and educated, expectations remain that lenders have a responsibility to take care of consumers.

They don't.

They have no responsibility to borrowers. Obviously as a borrower, if you go to a lender, you will be sold whatever they have. You need to understand who they are and what they do, but you're still responsible for your choices.

As I said earlier, in the big financial picture, banks provide needed resources. Canadian banks provide all the resources needed to source mortgages. Even if we go with a monoline lender, they are essentially using profit made from the branches. From there, they put that into investing in the monolines to ensure they have a piece of the market no matter which direction they take.

Understand that when you come to an independent mortgage professional, we're not bound to any particular bank. We're here to do the best for you under the circumstances provided. If you qualify, your mortgage professional can offer you several options. If you don't qualify, then you will be presented with whatever option works for you. We work hard to ensure the right fit, but it remains up to you to take the right direction in the first place.

Customers who do mortgages on their own at a bank see a nice financial advisor who's friendly and makes them feel good; they don't realize that—for the most part—an advisor merely inputs data. They don't approve the loans. Many customers believe they are sharing their stories with the people who are giving them the money, but that isn't the case. You either fit the program, or you don't; it isn't personal.

Mortgage advisors at banks aren't required to have a specific level of formal education, and you don't know if they're approving one loan, five loans, or five hundred loans. Besides that, loans aren't even their only area of expertise: they also open accounts, set payments, sell mutual funds, cross-sell insurance to other areas in the branch, and cross-sell financial advising. Advisors are rated on those sales, and it's far-fetched to believe they understand mortgages well enough to get you the best one. They'll do the best they can for you within that branch—we're not talking ill-will here—but that's it. Lenders have recognized that people want mortgage advisors, so many of them provide them. As a consumer, though, you need to understand the difference between mortgage advisors employed by a lender and a truly independent professional mortgage professional. The bank's advisor will always be biased in the bank's favour.

Again, I am not anti-bank, and you shouldn't be, either. I just want you to understand what a bank can and cannot offer you.

In 2017, employees from many of Canada's large institutions told CBC's Erica Johnson how they were pressured to upsell, trick, and even lie to customers to meet unrealistic sales targets and keep their jobs. The deluge of stories fuelled multiple calls for a parliamentary inquiry, even as the banks claimed they were acting in customers' best interests. In nearly one thousand emails, employees from locations across Canada described pressure to hit targets that are monitored weekly, daily, and in some cases hourly.

Customers don't think about it. The advisor is always nice to them and people tend to be trusting. But you don't know if the advisor lives in her mom's basement or if she owns ten properties. Her job is to sell. Does she know anything about being self-employed, for example? Does she know how to read financial statements? Does she understand profit and loss? Just because the advisors can see the deposits going into your bank account doesn't mean they understand the ebbs and flows of what's happening.

Again I come back to this fundamental truth: it's impossible to intelligently shop for a mortgage by yourself, and especially not online. These days, everybody starts their search online, and they think they know what to expect based on that experience. Don't do it! Those websites are created as bait. Despite what they say about simplicity and speed, the process is still the same, and they may or may not be connected to the resources that an independent mortgage professional can offer.

In addition, some mortgage offers are only for insured

mortgages, when you have less than a 20 percent down payment. Some are for certain amortizations that you may or may not qualify for, or might hurt your abilities down the road. One of the major banks had a great offer, but only if you transferred in $100,000 of investments. Do you know the difference? Can you sort through all those scenarios?

On top of that, if the advisor gets it wrong, your application is already flagged. A lot of banks insure mortgages on the back end, even if there's no paid insurance premium; that's how they package and sell loans. If the person who input the data for your mortgage didn't build the right story and connect all the dots or position your mortgage correctly because they missed something on the application, you're already in trouble. To be fair, maybe you weren't transparent because you didn't think to be, or you weren't asked the right questions. It doesn't really matter: either way, you're in trouble.

Lenders won't even look at documents until it's a real deal. This reinforces the problem around people wanting instant approval. Banks don't want to spend a lot of time on it—remember, only 10 to 12 percent of preapprovals go live—but borrowers want absolute certainty, and they want it right now.

Keep in mind, therefore, the lender needs an accepted

contract to even look at qualifying the property. The seller is not obligated to disclose anything until you do the same on your end. This sometimes rubs real estate agents the wrong way, but lenders won't look seriously at any property until it's an accepted deal.

I'm not trying to scare you away from a mortgage; that's the last thing I want to do. If you're thinking about buying a place, don't just think about it: do it. The tax benefits are extremely helpful, and the sooner you're in, the better. In most cases, you won't lose money, because if you can control your timing or there are restrictions on the home you've bought, you always have options with a home. Once you invest in real estate, it's the only investment you don't pay tax on when you sell (provided it's your principal residence) with the current tax law.

Replace "Should I?" with "How can I?"

Let me be clear: after fourteen years in this business working with some of the wealthiest people in the country, I've come to understand they know how to get their equity working for them. That's an option you only get when you own.

Independent mortgage professionals like my company have experience with lenders and can see the kinds of properties that have worked for them in the past. We can learn details and information that you'd never have access to. And there are more possible scenarios than you can imagine.

Sometimes, a lender will look at a property and just reject it outright. Sometimes, there's a long and complicated backstory. Someone else might have applied for a mortgage on the same property in the past, and the presence of an oil tank was disclosed; the new application says there's no oil tank, so the lender might require a report affirming there's currently no oil tank on the property.

The same thing holds true with various stratas (condos in the United States) that won't get into the meat and potatoes until everything is signed and done, because it costs money to do due diligence, and those forms have expiration dates as well: there's a shelf life to documentation. Every transaction is going to be different, and we're going to navigate through it in the most efficient manner that is going to result in the best, most accurate data.

Once there is an accepted offer in place after the initial preapproval, then we'll guide you through the next steps. We are part of your team to help you along the way!

HOW WELL DO YOU KNOW YOUR LENDER?

For most people, studying lender history presents more of

a challenge than deciphering a rocket ship's instruction manual! How long have they been in business? What do they do to attract new clients, and why do they want to? Is their existing base happy? How are they changing their policies?

A prime example of changing policies is around prepayment. One of the major banks we do business with changed its policies to remove terms that helped clients pay mortgages off faster, but it didn't put out any sort of announcement, making the change quietly and pretty much under the radar. When a client wanted to make a prepayment, they discovered that the bank's new policy only allowed them to prepay if they sold the property.

Lenders might even make an offer of a 10 percent prepayment, but without telling clients that this amazing offer is only good on one anniversary day.

In essence, if you can't prepay properly, you can be faced with future payment shock, higher costs down the road with unsecured debt to pay for things, or the requirement to pay a penalty to get a better mortgage, ultimately increasing your cost of borrowing. These are all reasons why we collaboratively assist you and help when you want to make prepayments so you have clarity on the whole picture. We're not saying it's bad to prepay your mortgage; it is important to have understanding and clarity on how to get things working for you, since your mortgage is generally a one-way street.

All lenders have their place, and people make decisions based on available intelligence and influences at the time. It's important to understand why banks do what they do. When banks have losses, they need to make up for it. In some cases, the way they choose to go about that walks a razor-thin line of integrity. A few banks will do things differently at different times, depending on the market.

In one instance, when the prime rate didn't change, one lender realized it could manipulate clients to the lender's advantage. This lender had losses in the United States it needed to compensate for through its Canadian operations. It decided to make its prime higher than any other banks, and not consistent with the Bank of Canada. It designed its variable rate mortgages to remain static, regardless of rates increasing or decreasing. A client's payment would not change, but the interest would. This lender took advantage of that client segment by increasing the interest rate and taking money from those clients' pockets. At the same time, the lender still offered new clients discounts compared to their competitors. Keep in mind that some clients like the benefit of this lender's product—that the payment doesn't change—but that will mean they can get out of touch with any changes.

Clients don't think about it and don't even know it's happening because their payment doesn't change. This is why we consistently review lender history. Whatever the circumstance was determined why you were placed with that lender at that time, but we look over your particular scenario to see if you can be in a more favourable mortgage. We can't control what the lenders will do, but we can always help and assist you in getting to the best place you can be.

PREFERRED AND MONOLINE LENDERS

The best mortgage professionals have preferred lenders, banks, and financial companies that work closely with the mortgage professional on a regular basis. These lenders know and trust the professional, so they often are able to give them better deals to offer clients. Monoline lenders only offer mortgage products and usually do not have storefronts; they're available primarily through the mortgage broker. Most of our preferred lenders are monoline lenders as well.

Mortgage professionals have access to dozens of lenders. It's important that we provide you with the top options based on your profile and needs. This keeps the Canadian mortgage market healthy, and at the lowest cost possible for the client.

PREFERRED LENDERS

If I'm able to put you with one of our preferred lenders, then I'll be able to be involved in your mortgage renewal, which is a tremendous benefit. These lenders don't have posted rates, or their posted rates are very close to their discounted rates, so you won't ever incur massive penalties. They'll give me better rates than they give to new clients, and—importantly—they'd rather treat their existing clients better and maintain that relationship over time. See why they're preferred?

Mortgages with low exit strategies are only available through mortgage brokers. They find the lender looking for the best applicants with the highest credit scores, the most provable income, the most prime properties, the best short bridge financing. There's a reason for their strict qualifications: when you need to make modifications to your mortgage, they're the best; they also are going to put the most money in your pocket. It may feel counterintuitive, but even if these lenders' interest rates are higher, it would be in your best interests to go with them if you could qualify for it. Look back to the $300,000 mortgage difference earlier in this chapter, which resulted in a savings of $15,000.

Can you think of a time in your life when you wouldn't appreciate an extra $15,000?

If you qualify and it's consistent with your wealth-building strategy, then that's where we'll try to get you in first. That's our number-one goal. If you can't qualify, or it's not suited for the timing based on all factors, then we'll go with a different lender.

And then there are circumstances in which we have to

use a lender that might not be preferred but is best for particular scenarios. It could be the client's credit score is too low at that time. It could be a problem with income and they need exceptions. It could be the timing, the property type, or the amount they need to take out. In spite of obstacles, our number-one goal is to put you with the best possible lender. Most of the time we'll be going to a bank, but when you're going through us, you'll have all the information in hand: we'll tell you what they don't.

An example of a situation where it's best to use an alternate lender is a one-day subject removal. This is simply a matter of timing, when a client says, "I need my answer right now." If you need your answer in a specific time frame, then we have to look at the resources around us and see who can commit in that time frame.

Everyone has different priorities. There are people who are in a hurry, and we're willing to facilitate what it is that they want, as long as they understand the consequences of their decisions. If you want to put an offer together next week, and your mortgage professional doesn't have all the documents to get it approved, it's not going to happen.

JILL'S INTEREST RATE ADVENTURE

One example of what I can do is this: when you're up for renewal, I'll always look for what your best options are;

I'll always do what's best for you. Jill was an insurance broker excited about an interest rate advertisement she'd seen, and she contacted us to begin the mortgage process. A short while later, she found an advertisement for a different but equally amazing interest rate while surfing the web. She called us and said she didn't need our help anymore because she got a far better rate somewhere else.

In effect, my reply was, "I doubt that option's in your best interest: we would have offered it if it were a good option." What I was thinking was, I guess we'll hear from you when that falls apart. Obviously, if it had been in her best interest, we would have already told her to go there. She wasted three weeks and an additional payment on her high-interest credit cards and debt going down this path, only to find out the offer wasn't applicable to her. It was the typical bait and switch—you don't qualify for this, but hey, we've got this other product for you.

After all was said and done, of course, we received an email from Jill. "Yeah, you were right. It was too good to be true. How do we proceed?" We went ahead with an approval and saved her some money, and then Jill asked, "What about when my mortgage is up for renewal? Do I have to go through this whole process again?"

I said, "Absolutely. The lender that we put you with is likely the best lender for you, but I can't guarantee that will be the same in the future. We'll still do the work to search and evaluate the market to ensure you have the best."

We had to put the information in front of her so she could connect the dots. She ended up walking away with one of the best mortgages in the country, with the best lender, and with the best exit strategy. Provided her life continues down that road and she doesn't need to make any modifications, and the lender sends us the renewal documents to review, she should be in great shape for the long term.

But we don't take that for granted. We continue to work with our clients to ensure they have the best option, because so many things can happen in anyone's life as well as in the lender market. I never take it for granted because I think their finances are too important.

WHOLESALE VERSUS RETAIL MORTGAGES

The best analogy here is a big-box store versus a specialized retailer. Lenders with the best rates and terms deal with wholesale. All my company does is mortgages, and we send big lenders those mortgages. Who do you think gets better pricing? If I need to buy a case of toilet paper, where will I get the better deal? At Costco or a corner store?

In terms of customer service, the best independent

mortgage professionals will supply the customer service experience with the savings of a big-box store!

DOUG'S LIGHT-BULB MOMENT

Doug was a buyer for a building supply company. We did a mortgage for him and he fully understood the scoop. Like most people, Doug had always dealt with banks for his mortgage needs; he'd worked with banks for the better part of the past thirty years. But he had listened to my radio show, and when his mortgage was up for renewal, he called in.

Doug said, "You know, Angela, I totally get it. I'm a buyer for a supply company. Someone coming in off the street won't get the same price as someone who buys hundreds of thousands of dollars' worth of flooring. As a consumer, you just won't get the same price as a wholesaler. I totally got it when you explained that on the show, and I wondered how much money I've lost over the past three decades by doing my own mortgages."

He added, "I really don't believe anyone thinks about

that when it comes to mortgages." This illustration gives weight to the fact that people tend to think of financial products in a different category than other products.

MONOLINE LENDERS

If you want the best money-saving mortgage, it often comes from a monoline lender. They get their business from one place only: mortgage brokers. Monolines have the strictest policies and they work with clients that best fit their models.

Monolines want to deal with something when it's live and favour A1 clients and A1 properties. They're not competitive in the preapproval space; they offer the best exit and renewal terms. Since they depend on mortgage brokers for their business, they don't have high costs and associated fees.

We do our very best to match the right client with the right lender—preferred, monoline, credit union, insurance company, or bank. But what happens if you don't qualify for any of the available options? We have a mortgage for you, too. If you don't qualify for it right now, we're still here for you; we'll show you what you need to do so that you can qualify in the future. We'll work out a plan together to get you there. We take our relationship with our clients seriously, and we want to be with you through your lifetime of purchasing property.

CHAPTER FOUR

MORTGAGE BROKERS ARE NOT ALL THE SAME

Just as no two snowflakes are alike, mortgage lending companies all have unique qualities. In this chapter I'm going to be talking briefly about my team, but what I'll be saying can apply to other top-tier mortgage professionals as well. The best professionals have core values and beliefs that set them apart from others, who know each lender's qualities and drawbacks, and who know how to match them with the right client...who may even be you.

When you want something done, you ask someone who knows how to do it. It's really that simple. My team's experience and values are the reasons we're in the business: we know how to do mortgages. There are only a handful of groups in the country that do the same volume of mortgages we do. The more experience you have, the more you refine your systems to provide consistently top-shelf service.

I'm fortunate to have a unique perspective on the marketplace, because I'm in both the business of mortgages and real estate investing, and also in the media business. As a media personality, I analyze and deliver data to consumers in an entertaining and informative manner, so they have a clear understanding of how to take advantage of the market at hand. I regularly offer different strategies and viewpoints on how to best utilize information. And that's what you need to look for in choosing your own mortgage team: an ability to see the big picture.

To illustrate, let's say you're on an airplane, and the plane hits turbulence, bouncing and bucking like a bronco with a caffeine buzz. The seat belt light comes on and the captain tells everyone to put their tray tables up because you're in for a rough ride. Will you feel safer with a pilot who's on his fifth flight, or one who's done 5,000?

And it's not just the years of experience that brokers like us bring to the table. There have been several times throughout the last decade and a half where things have come out in the media, or even speculative information—news that needed to be disseminated. When provided with the option, we advised our clients of these situations before we advised our associates or the media.

I've always felt it's a big responsibility to do somebody's mortgage, and it is most definitely a collaborative effort, with everyone on the team—the client, the lender, the real estate agent, and the mortgage professional—doing their part. I love knowing that I'm taking that responsibility seriously and am doing things right, establishing and building rewarding relationships with clients that lead to positive moments in their lives.

We have a winning system and implementation strategy, and while this book is meant to help you navigate the pitfalls of mortgage borrowing, it can't replace having a seasoned and successful mortgage professional on your side.

In this business, you always have to adapt and execute based on what's in front of you. I have developed a unique and effective model with proven and tested strategies, but perhaps the brightest advantage is instinct. I bring clarity amidst chaos to execute our model to the fullest benefit for our clients.

COMPETITOR BRAND MORTGAGE BROKERS VERSUS ANGELA

Every day, mortgage brokers come and go. At the young age of thirty-five, I have the fire of youth combined with fourteen years experience in the industry, and I'm just getting warmed up! Most people are just ramping up their careers in their thirties. I've already established an enviable and successful track record of helping clients. While most brokers' responsibility is to simply get you a mortgage, I will be here to continue to help people navigate their mortgages for many years to come.

Every mortgage brokerage office is independently owned and operates on individual business models. Many of them are unaware of, or don't ask, the right questions. We engage with clients at a deeper level to uncover exactly what it is they need and find the best way to get it. That's one of the reasons we've had so much success and is testament to our passion for helping Canadians through financial challenges. We're in this together: it's a partnership.

That concept is key. We're not in it alone: our clients are key to our success. They know (and after reading his book, you should as well) that a successful mortgage application is a collaborative process. If a client doesn't receive a document, or has a question, they reach out to us: the communication is a two-way street. We are all in this together, and we reach our goals through a partnership.

My team is made up of highly trained professionals licensed by the Financial Institutions Commission. We are required to pursue continuing education in the field, and we do so eagerly. Clients can feel confident working with any member of the team. I oversee everything, but I don't review initial documents or field the initial phone call to our office. I have been known to hop into that role when volume demands, but I must focus on the operation as a whole to ensure superior service.

That will be true of any efficient mortgage company. Restaurant owners know how to delegate clearing the tables, cooking the food, and doing the dishes. They wouldn't be successful if they couldn't delegate. The same concept applies to any successful business.

BANKS VERSUS ANGELA

In the banking world, there are no licensing requirements to become a mortgage banker. You go through sales training, and then you input data for someone else to review and approve.

Is that really comforting? It's like an adult game of telephone. There are educated people in the industry, but it's difficult for them to stay on top of things because of their sheer size. They may have 10,000 employees. Compare that with the three people who are on my team!

As I've already mentioned, independent mortgage professionals have a deeper understanding of mortgages and how they work, where to go, and how to get them done. We are proactive; banks are reactive. A banker's target review and opportunity for advancement is based on cross-selling the most profitable products, whereas a great mortgage professional simply wants to save you money.

This showed up over the last decade when lines of credit went up to prime plus one, which means that adjustable-rate loans fluctuated to one point above prime. Everybody got a letter in the mail informing them of this change in credit. But nobody got a letter when all the banks decided to reduce their lines of credit by half a percent. Our team reached out to all of our clients, saying, "Hey, this is what's happening in the industry. There could be an opportunity to save you money. Let's collaborate and see what the best option is."

We always demonstrate our experience because we don't want you to have to refinance all the time. I just got an email from a client who was doing a home renovation. Back last year, I'd said to this client, "Look. Take out more money. Trust me. You're saying you won't spend it and you need a six-month emergency fund. If it doesn't work, we have this mortgage for you where you can put all that money back." The client didn't listen to me, and the email I just received from them says, "We should have listened to you. Now we have to break the mortgage again because we're running short on our renovation, and at this point I might not even qualify to get the money."

We take the long view for all our clients. We can do that because all we do is mortgages. Banks would love to give you a credit card or a line of credit or even some insurance, because they make more money from higher rates and fees. We don't have anybody looking over our shoulder saying, "How come you didn't sell ten credit cards this month?"

BEING PROACTIVE

We want to give you power and control over your equity and your financial future.

Being proactive is an important part of who we are and what we do. We don't have a job description dictating what sales we have to make. Our salaries aren't based on sales of particular products. We are not here to be reactive; we are here to be proactive whenever possible.

Every day I pull reports to see if there's an opportunity to save people money. That gives me a start, but even though the numbers might say I don't have an opportunity to save you money, I'll still check in with you because maybe there might be something going on in your life that we can use to your advantage. That's why we do annual reviews, reminding you to get in touch with us so we can connect and ensure everything's going in the right direction.

We also have a strategy in place to protect you from future

payment shock, because we know that interest rates right now are low, but they won't always stay that way. Not only are we here to help you plan your mortgage and optimize the market, but we're here to help you protect your equity as well. We consistently review your mortgage and options to help you do that. Unless someone is doing that proactively, how can you possibly save money? When was the last time your bank called and said, "I think I've found a way to save you more money?"

Our process is unique among independent mortgage brokers. We understand the entire process, from home buying to mortgage financing to mortgage funding. There are no layers of staff with different knowledge and oversight capabilities, and we remain fully transparent. We are very black-and-white and use only one application to shop lenders. That way we can protect clients' credit and place them with the best available product for the long term.

We don't speculate about what might or might not happen; we don't make any assumptions. We come in, do our initial review, and invest the time, money, energy, and expertise needed to thoroughly review your scenario. Whatever the result of that review, we will then provide options and advice. There's no point in talking about what you qualify for, or what kinds of rates are out there, until we've reviewed all the documentation. The documentation will dictate the best move, and your credit will represent three-quarters of the review. If there is a property already involved, then of course we will go through that process as well.

Again, don't go after rates, especially if they're advertised aggressively. Take the same time to explore your options with a mortgage professional that you'd take for consultation with a medical professional. At the time of writing this book, I don't even have rates advertised on my website. Be cautious in selecting the team you work with. Do you think the top professionals in the business are willing to jump through hoops, to drive across town at dinnertime to go over your options with you? Anyone without a system and a process might not be the best team for you. If you're getting the best people in the industry, they have a process that doesn't involve sitting at your kitchen table with all kinds of distractions. Is that where Warren Buffett evaluates hedge funds?

Lenders do the best and most efficient work for clients who are properly positioned by mortgage professionals. Most clients don't think about that; they just want someone to give them a quick answer. Someone with quick answers doesn't necessarily make for the right fit. Just because you like how someone looks on a first date doesn't mean it will be the person you marry. It might happen, but the likelihood of love at first sight is pretty slim.

REAL-TIME STRATEGIES

Our business model, skills, and beliefs allow us to keep pace with changes and adapt to a client's needs. On one client's signing day, something in the marketplace changed, and we responded immediately with a change to the strategy and the approval, which ended up being financially beneficial for the client to the tune of tens of thousands of dollars. Because we're independent and can move quickly, we have everything we need to accommodate clients.

Think about how information travels in the bank. Think about how many people have to be trained and taught to understand a change of strategy and what that implementation process will be. A big bank can have tens of thousands of employees to keep abreast of changes, where we have our own team. Looking at volume and terms, because everyone here has the same education level and understanding of how we do things, we can be very agile and responsive to clients' needs.

Think about it. If a surgeon has just done three unexpected emergency procedures back to back and hasn't slept for three days, do you really want them taking on your heart surgery? You want someone fresh, with the ability to think clearly and give you their best. That's what you get with an independent mortgage professional.

We automatically adjust our processes to best serve clients.

Neither side really needs to think about the process; it just gets done. Circumstances will take us to different places based on the market, timing, qualifications, and your life stage. That sets the baseline; everything else derives from what happens with those components. If the situation requires us to secure your mortgage with a lender who's not preferred, we still always check every detail to help you move forward.

OUR CORE VALUES WORK FOR YOU

My team is here to do the best for you, whether that means we'll do business or not. If we can't help you now, then we'll help you in the future. Some prospective clients seem to think we should fight for their business. That's not how we work. If we're going to be here to help you for the next five years, we must have a good working relationship.

I've written pretty extensively about this for the *Globe and Mail* and other publications: if you have half a million dollars in the stock market, there's a very regimented system to understand how that money is monitored and what's being reviewed to ensure you're consistently optimizing the market. I feel the same about mortgages. I got into this business so everyone could get the most savings possible, not only one class of people. Everyone deserves that opportunity when it comes to financing, and that's why I'm a mortgage professional. I have a love and respect for anyone who works hard to accomplish their goals. It doesn't matter how much money you make; I'm here to help you the same way, and ensure you have the same options.

I am here to do what is best for you, not what is best for me. Financial balance makes for less stress in your personal life, less stress on your mental and physical health, and perhaps less stress on your marriage. People have enough of those problems to deal with already, and we feel we contribute to society by doing the best we can for people. The best mortgage professionals out there feel the same way.

BREAKING THE MORTGAGE CODE

CHAPTER FIVE

THE BORROWER'S RESPONSIBILITIES

As a borrower and client in this highly productive and collaborative relationship, you have to be able to carry your weight, and you have to be accountable. You need to understand your role, be completely transparent, and assume everything matters.

But the truth is you can't do better until you know better. The borrower's engagement and accountability are crucial for thorough mortgage intelligence.

We can use analogies of building a house, playing sports, or staying healthy. If you build a house on the strength of a solid foundation, it's much easier to do it quickly and effectively. The house will remain strong for years to come. If you're a tennis buff, you cannot improve your skills by playing with a beginner. You want to play with someone who will challenge you and elevate your abilities. If you're looking to become as healthy as you can possibly be, you have to be transparent with your health records and what you are doing in order to work collaboratively with a trainer or physician to improve.

It's the same with mortgages. It's not that people are simply silly or uneducated; it's just life. As a general rule, we have to exercise a great deal of effort just to meet our daily responsibilities. People are overwhelmed, and it can be easy to overlook mundane but critical details. An example of this is someone might change their contact information and forget to let us know. We won't be able to communicate with them, and they get upset because they didn't hear from us. Some people have actually changed bank accounts and forgotten about their mortgage payment or didn't realize they had to contact their lender.

Other things change, too. Some families go from two earners to one for a variety of reasons—staying home to care for children, being laid off, looking after a family member. We know these changes happen, but it's important for you to be proactive in letting us know when they do.

Because we understand all those stresses, my team has systems in place to triple-check things. We initially set you up with a payment plan, with a payment amount determined by the strategy in place. Thirty days after completion, we'll send you an email asking you to verify everything has gone as anticipated. Whenever humans or computers are involved, there will be errors, so we send that reminder for you to check everything on your end.

Your mortgage payment is essential, and generally that's everybody's first priority; but what about other types of insurance payments? How do you decide to pay those? Most of us just spend our money, and we don't look at where it's going; but once you have additional investments, you want to make sure. Reviewing your bank statements is a really good practice. Some people learn they've been paying unnecessary insurance for years because they haven't done the simple task of reviewing their bank statement.

Part of your responsibility is being aware of timing. If you are in a variable-rate mortgage, the timing of locking in is very important. Some lenders allow us to assist with the locking-in portion of the mortgage; some do not. If you get a mortgage through some lenders, you have to go directly to that bank and make arrangements with them, though you can always consult with us to see if you should or should not proceed.

We can only do what we can do to the best of our ability. Again, I have no control over the banks, but obviously we have had influence on them and that can be advantageous to clients. In times of high volume when there is a change, we have systems in place to notify people in advance. However, if you've been away for two months, rates have gone up, and if you've received notice but haven't reached out to the lender or us, you can't be upset if you miss an opportunity. Some things in your life happen quickly, and we won't know about it unless you tell us. Remember our airline pilot example? There might be unexpected turbulence in your life; we can help navigate but only if we have weather updates!

Based on the different factors we've seen evolve over the past thirty years, I really believe we're living in a radically changed economic reality. In the past, the economy was dealing with worker supply and demand issues that aren't relevant any longer because of changes in technology and product sourcing. We used to live in an economy where things were locally sourced, and now products are sourced all over the world. The takeaway here? As technology evolves, we'll find better ways to use it. The mortgage market will continue to evolve.

A PROSPECTIVE CLIENT'S FRAMEWORK

We ask a lot of questions upfront so we can establish an efficient strategy and ensure clients understand they're the ones making the decisions. To be honest, a lot of people aren't comfortable with that: they want us to tell them what to do!

Part of your responsibility is to be forthcoming with your information and assume everything matters. If I tell you my opinion and you feel otherwise, that's fine; we'll help you execute whatever you decide to do. If you ask for our expert opinion, realize it might change based on your circumstances. The most intelligent and informed people want to understand both sides of the coin and make a decision based on what they feel is in their best interest.

When a doctor gives you a prescription, they don't follow you around to verify you're taking it all the time. That's up to you. Some doctors will ask more questions than others to get to the root of the issue; it's the same with us. Sometimes we don't even need to ask because we can see it clearly, but we have a framework in place that determines the best strategy for you. Everyone's situation is different in respect to their needs, wants, and life stage. The mortgage we get for them today will not be the same one they will have throughout their life. We'll adapt based on the market and changing life scenarios, and it's especially critical to monitor anything that changes relating to credit, income, and habitation.

I recently heard from a smart, educated person who wanted advice and help with his strategy, but he didn't really know what he wanted to do with his money. He said, "I have $200,000. What should I do? Should I invest in the market, or should I invest in real estate?"

In the real world, people seek advice from a myriad of sources: a financial planner, their mom, or the barista at the coffee shop. If you come to me, I'll use my experience to demonstrate what I think to be the best way. In most cases, if you go to a financial planner, they will suggest something that profits them. They don't get paid to give you advice that doesn't profit them and it's their job to manage your assets. You need to be prepared with a thorough review of your scenario. I always suggest first talking to your accountant. They can analyze what you are doing for retirement, tax efficiency, and planning for the future, providing you have an accountant with substantial real estate experience, which I always advise.

I knew this person wanted to grow his wealth as soon as possible. My recommendation was not to put the money down on their mortgage since their mortgage was actually a rental. He travelled a lot for business and ended up renting out the place, and the rent covered the mortgage. He can only get that money out of his mortgage if he needed it by selling or refinancing the property. I suggested he first and foremost look at tax efficiency and safety planning. From there, he could look at a dividend-paying investment that obviously could be real estate. The loan-to-value will determine if you are getting additional cash flow or not. This client is very successful, but I always advise against investing every single penny and stretching yourself too thin.

When you have questions about your finances and you ask a wide assortment of people for advice, you can easily get more confused than when you started. You play the starring role in your decision-making, however. You have to understand and look at everything, and have clarity based on what is good for you.

THE TEACHER AND THE ARCHITECT

Let's look at an example illustrating why borrowers need to remain engaged in the process. Sam and Julie from Vancouver were looking at a new home and heard of our agency through Julie's mom. They planned to contact us for preapproval but didn't get around to it, and so we got their information in a sudden belated deluge of documents.

We worked quickly to get information in the system so we could position them properly, and then we started shopping the mortgage around. We discovered that they'd already shopped with multiple mortgage brokers in Canada. That process takes points off your credit score, causes unnecessary scrutiny of your account, and affects your rate. Most importantly, it alerts lenders to watch for your file because of potential fraud.

Most customers are unaware that lenders look closely at things like this. Lenders believe customers should have already selected a mortgage broker to work with before submitting their file. If that hasn't happened, it's usually because the client is modifying their application in the hopes of getting a better result somewhere else. Lenders have obligations to tell the broker what is going on, because they don't offer the same commitment to two different mortgage professionals. If you happen to have a tight time frame, it also delays getting your approval.

This isn't the way to do business. If we'd known the client was applying to multiple agencies, we wouldn't have committed so many hours to reviewing and working with their file. The clients didn't get what they wanted, and the lenders looked in askance at us for not being on top of the clients' information, so no one was happy.

Because of examples like that one, we won't work with clients who aren't transparent or who don't use us exclusively with their file, and you'll find that most reputable brokers feel the same. We cannot do the best job for them, and the process ultimately costs Canadian taxpayers, because when lenders have to spend money putting out fires instead of just underwriting the file, it increases their costs and the public ends up paying.

If you don't allow us to represent you properly, we cannot put our reputation on the line for you. We were talking about this recently with one of our clients who is a heart surgeon. He compared this scenario to the operating room. "I am the person doing the surgery and calling out the orders in respect to what I need to be able to do at a very critical time. I couldn't imagine if I had four heart surgeons all trying to get in there and do the same thing! One person has to take the lead and do what they need to do."

Some mortgage brokers don't insist on transparency, but we're not afraid of losing a client who won't follow the process. We're here to work with thorough and committed clients. We need to know if you've done something with your file or worked with someone else, someone less educated or less experienced, or if you've been declined somewhere. If you can be honest with us, then we're happy to help you. We understand that at any given time people do the best they can with the information they have. We can help you fix a problem, but we need to know about it.

OUR CLIENTS COME FIRST

I am fortunate to be in a position that helps my clients. I am constantly monitoring the market and staying attuned to changes in it, and because of that, I consider myself something of an early warning system to my clients. Before I announce anything new in the media affecting mortgages, my clients have already heard about it and benefitted from that early knowledge.

I go back to the analogy of taking care of our own family and our own health first. We see early market indicators through a variety of sources, including sitting in on lender and insurer panels, and when we do, our clients benefit from that information in the earliest stages. As long as we understand the issues—and it can take time to understand the issues at hand—we can advise them in advance. After informing our clients, we contact associates who've signed up for our newsletter, and it's only then that we release our findings to the media.

In an airplane, if a situation arises where passengers need to access the oxygen masks, it's paramount to secure your own before helping anybody else. That's what we're doing. We're taking care of our clients first and the public second.

CHAPTER SIX

WHAT YOU NEED TO KNOW BEFORE WE MEET

Congratulations! You've made the decision to reach out to our team. We look forward to meeting new clients, and I personally work with my team on initial steps and overall strategies. What can you expect, and what can you do to prepare for the process?

It's important that you feel confident with our operation and staff. My team is fully committed to satisfying every detail of your mortgage needs. The entire team operates with the same core values and the same integrity, and executes the same success strategies.

A CONVERSATION

The first step is a five-minute conversation to learn

about your goals and needs. You can contact us through the contact link on our website, or directly at callateam@dominionlending.ca, or call us. We'll learn a little about what your life looks like right now: your work environment, your methods of income, and where you want to go financially. Based on that information, we'll send you a list of what we need to more fully assess your situation.

Once this additional information is in place, we'll process and review it for clarity. Throughout this discovery process, we look for any mistakes from the credit bureau and note anything we can do to enhance your position with lenders or with your particular circumstance.

In general, if you live within twenty-five kilometres or so of our office, we'll meet with you in person. We'll present you with your options and proceed from there. A lot of people we help live in the interior or on the island, and if that's the case, we can do a meeting over the phone where we review everything line item by line item, and then make recommendations from there.

Those recommendations might not include closing your loan immediately. We might recommend that you wait for a specific time or upcoming life circumstance. There will probably be a few options available that will offer you the best results, and discussing them before we've had the opportunity to evaluate everything is a waste of time. Everyone's scenario is different, the market is always in flux, and sometimes as we work through the process we learn that we need to take a different direction or require further information.

We will continue to collaboratively work together, ask questions, and learn about your situation to present the best option when that time comes. If, on the other hand, we identify that it is not best for you to move forward, we will let you know and suggest alternatives.

UNDERSTANDING OUR HIGH-LEVEL STRATEGY

I've heard it said that mortgage professionals ask too many questions and require too much documentation. If there's one piece of advice I hope you take from this book, it's that there's a strategy behind everything a professional mortgage specialist requires and it's in your best interests to cooperate with that strategy.

We will ask clients for different documents at various times throughout the process. The truth is that most mortgage professionals hate paperwork and only require what is needed! It's still a necessary component of our job and so it has to be taken very seriously. There are a number of ways the mortgage process can go and we need to ensure, from both compliance and positioning perspectives, that we have everything we asked for presented in the proper order.

Some documents and information have a shelf life, and that's why we sometimes might not ask for everything upfront. For instance, pay stubs, bank statements, and letters of employment have a thirty-day shelf life. If we feel the process will go beyond those thirty days, we will look to complete everything in such a way that we only have to do it once, unless for some reason it's more advantageous to provide some items twice.

We understand everyone experiences a certain amount of anxiety associated with the mortgage application process. We'll move forward together most productively when we can ask you questions and establish a working baseline.

Remember that what we request is from a compliance perspective, and there's nothing we can do about those items; there's no flexibility. At particular times in the course of the loan, inquiries can come from the lender, who reserves the right to ask for anything at any time, including additional documents, and they can pull approvals at the last minute if they need to.

Sometimes, lenders' requests can be unexpected and unsettling, but it helps to understand that they have audits going on in the background themselves. We might have received a complete file, and then, the day before you're moving, they could ask for a pay stub or some other documentation even though we've already met all their requirements, for any number of reasons. It could be a random audit on their end. Maybe the person who approved the file left the organization, and now the lenders are reviewing their decisions. Anything can happen, but we're experienced at dealing with these scenarios and you have the most experienced pilot to navigate these stressful waters.

In spite of our experience, and even if we do everything by the book, problems may come up. It's unusual, but it happens. Remember we are here by your side to do whatever we can to help you move forward. Again, this is a collaborative process, so if a crisis does arise, the best frame of mind is to spend time on the what rather than on the why. What do I need to do next?

I'm thinking of a self-employed graphic designer, who was seeking preapproval. In this particular instance, the designer approached us and said, "I'm already preapproved at my bank. I just want to see if I can do better."

"That's great," I replied. "Here's an outline of all the documents we'll need prior to assisting you and letting you know your options."

He was totally shocked. "What? Why would I need all these documents? I didn't get asked for all that when I got preapproved."

"Well, then you're not preapproved. How is it possible to preapprove you if they haven't looked at all the necessary documents that play a role in actually determining the outcome?"

I always assume outside sources review everything, but we still get calls from people who thought they were preapproved, or thought things were okay, and then there were problems because the lender hadn't actually reviewed all the details. I presented an analogy to the designer to help him understand: "Could you design a logo for someone if you knew nothing about their company values, what they're looking to portray, their history, or what vision they have in place?"

He said, "Of course I couldn't, that makes perfect sense." It's so important to plan ahead and follow a strategy. Would you rather build a house on sand or have the concrete poured before you start framing the walls? Do you want to find clarity on the plan before you execute it, or do you want to execute the plan and then be constantly stuck in frustration going back to fix things?

MORTGAGES AND MATERNITY

Pregnant? Thinking about becoming pregnant? Just had a baby? Congratulations! Adding on to your family can be a tremendous blessing, but it comes with a certain amount of stress as well.

The reduction of income and all the new financial pressure of your family's growing expenses can feel daunting, so preparing yourself for the future using the right mortgage strategy can help.

There are some common misconceptions about maternity and your mortgage, the most significant being that many lenders won't recognize your income. Different lenders have different policies and use different percentages of your pre-maternity income. What they decide will depend on your credit score (which your independent mortgage professional protects by using one application to shop multiple lenders) and equity in your home.

If you are pregnant when you buy your home, or upon review of your mortgage, you'll need a strategy to help you pay your mortgage off faster yet have your payment reduced when your income is reduced. It's easy to feel overwhelmed while you and your baby are learning about your new life together, but an early consultation with a mortgage professional will help.

THE SELF-EMPLOYED CLIENT

When I started the Angela Calla Mortgage Team, I worked through all the struggles, dreams, and rewards that are part of running a business. I know what it takes to be an entrepreneur and how disciplined you have to be when you have aggressive goals to be the best you can be.

A mortgage broker's most common clients are self-employed workers such as instructors at universities. People generating income from multiple sources also benefit from a broker relationship. For example, a plumber working full-time for a company might also do jobs on the side. Who are we kidding? These days, everyone needs to have a side hustle or to make money from their passion products. I've noticed that a lot of people I know are creating or doing things they love that help them earn a living, at least in part. They make jewellery, essential oils, or candles. Artists create and sell art; musicians play gigs. I recently met a man who owns a Benjamin Moore franchise but also plays in a band; he loves music, and why not get paid for doing what you love? My father plays the accordion and would probably love to get paid for it...hey, did you know he's available for private parties? Accordionist, anyone?

Brokers like me understand their lifestyle. Self-employed people generally have various ways of driving their income based on tax advice and their company's cash flow. I simply don't believe that someone familiar only with a nine-to-five job, who has never had self-employed income or multiple streams of income, can fully understand and provide the best solution for these people.

We can go back to the example of learning from the most successful people. If you want to get the most and best mortgage terms, go to a self-employed expert rather than to a lender where someone who works on salary offers whatever they happen to have. With the lender's employee, either you fit in the box or you don't. In the latter case, you wasted a lot of time, money, and resources to essentially bang your head against the wall.

Once we understand how you're driving your income, we know exactly what lenders want to see. If mortgage brokers don't represent you properly, or ask the right questions to determine a solution, you could have a setback that could take months or years to reverse, so if you're self-employed it's critical to align yourself with someone who understands how best to portray your income.

Every lender has limitations on dealing with self-employed people. It's easy to think that because you have a business account at a certain bank and they're able to see the money flowing in and out of that account, then that bank will be more likely to give you a mortgage. That doesn't matter. The lenders work with specific products.

Just because a bank sees your money coming in and going out doesn't mean they have the best solution for you. In fact, this might come as a surprise, but even people who manage large portfolios with lenders generally don't go to those lenders for their own mortgages.

Self-employed clients always need to be aware and very careful. Many mortgages are back-end insured, so the same one or two agencies see the same application. If for some reason the application is declined, it could be a year or more before they're willing to overturn their decision. We know what lenders want to see to approve a certain type of loan for self-employed or multiple-stream income clients. Early in the process, we can advise on what you'll need to show in terms of income, or the best method for portraying your income, so that you can get where you want to be.

Depending on what type of mortgage you're willing to consider, we can also offer alternative options if you aren't anxious to show as much income as a traditional lender would like to see. There are alternative lenders better suited for that scenario. These lenders will give you a mortgage at a higher interest rate, but a lot of self-employed borrowers prefer to take the higher interest rates instead of paying more money in taxable income.

Vicky is one of our self-employed clients. She owned

a vehicle repair shop that showed very little money on paper, and she far preferred to pay a 2 percent higher interest rate than to pay extra tens of thousands of dollars in income taxes.

This is just one of many different scenarios that someone with expertise can guide you through when they specialize in working with self-employed people. And if there's a solution available that we don't have access to, we'll always be honest with you and guide you in the direction best suited to your situation and your needs.

A SELF-EMPLOYED WORKER'S BEST OPTION

In addition to understanding the self-employed culture by like-minded association, mortgage brokers specialize in understanding your financials and taking the time to learn the ins and outs of your business.

A key tool in this regard is our self-employment questionnaire.

This questionnaire helps ensure that all your options have been evaluated. Situations differ significantly depending on your profession, on whether or not you have an actual location, on whether you're mainly a subcontractor, on whether you work with a consistent client set, and on many other variables.

One of my clients, Cheryl, owned a marketing company that worked mainly with developers. She was moving her physical location from Victoria to Vancouver; she had a contract with developers there for several years' duration. In Vancouver, she planned to use a condo she'd purchased from one of her clients as her office to save money, money that could be taken off the financials as an expense and put into the mortgage.

Those contracts and the information regarding her location and activity allowed her to obtain a better mortgage than she'd initially thought she could. My team understood what lenders were looking for in this case, and our ability to be proactive helped Cheryl understand what needed to happen for her to accomplish her goal.

Individual lenders, on the other hand, typically have no idea how to advise in scenarios like this. They only look at incoming transactions but don't understand the inherent fundamentals. Staff members have a certain number of products to offer, and they focus on sales, not financials.

We understand those things from a financial perspective and present accordingly, so the likelihood of you getting the mortgage you need increases significantly. If you go somewhere that only has one product, even if that product could enhance your positioning, how do you know there isn't somewhere else that can get you a better product?

You never know until you go to an unbiased source with specialized experience.

SELF-EMPLOYED? WHAT YOU NEED TO KNOW

I won't lie to you: self-employed financials are tricky. Most mortgage professionals like to see multiple years of financials, because lenders look for patterns (a change in profit from one year to another, inconsistent balances, a big change as a result of accounting practices or sale of assets, or rapid growth). Any changes need to be noted in order to provide clarity to a lender. Sometimes, it will be best to wait based on the current situation or what you can show on your financials. Your mortgage professional will invest the time to consult with you and ensure you are ideally positioned.

Sometimes, it's just not the right time and you'll have to re-evaluate what you need to do to eventually get the mortgage that provides you the most benefit. Once those changes are made, you can move forward accordingly.

This is exactly what happened with one of our current clients in Port Coquitlam. The wife is self-employed and the husband is a firefighter; they had two pre-teenaged kids, a baby, and an upcoming wedding to finance. The one-year anniversary of their mortgage wasn't until July, so we started consulting with them in January.

We told them, "This is the kind of money you will need to show, and this is the amount you will have to pay off in income taxes beforehand to make it work." That gave them six months to show the required revenue and income and pay their income tax. That also matched up with the anniversary date of their mortgage so we were able to make a change. These clients were patient, followed our advice, and found the result they wanted.

The results saved them $1,600 a month that they're now saving and using to invest in RESPs, RRSPs, a wedding, and an investment property, and they're moving toward being real estate investors with their newfound savings, just to name a few of the benefits.

DOCUMENTATION NEEDS

In addition to general information on the state of your business, we need a collection of detailed documents to move forward with the mortgage process. These documents can include the following:

- Pay stub or other documentation of income
- Last two years' notice of assessment from income tax (called "income tax return" in the US)
- Documentation of all additional sources of income
- Child support or other outgoing income responsibilities

- Full version of T1 Generals
- Notice of Articles of Ownership

If you have multiple jobs, or work in an industry that pays hourly, be prepared to provide the last two years of T4s and maybe a year-end pay stub. I'll also want to know about the NOAs[5] and T1s, depending on the mortgage closing date compared to when we analyze the updated T1s. An assessment might be required depending on the time of the year and your particular circumstance.

That list gives you an idea of what we'll need. In most cases it's easier to work with an accountant; some people associate an accountant with just another bill to pay, but in fact it's the opposite—your accountant not only saves you money but has everything easily available on a PDF file and can email it over in a couple of moments.

Some people have multiple companies. Some people have an operating company, a holding company, and a family trust. The different layers in law will determine the documentation required, and it can get very complex. Your accountant can help you sort through it all for your mortgage application.

---

5   In Canada, this is a Notice of Assessment, an annual statement sent to taxpayers detailing their tax account status.

OTHER INCOME

If you work for a company, be sure the letter of employment they give you is up-to-date. It should state your current position, length of employment, and amount you're paid. The lender will call the employer every single time. If you're getting a letter for your mortgage provider, let your employer know they'll be called so there aren't any delays. In addition, be sure the contact at your place of employment is absolutely certain of the information. The lender will want to confirm every detail in an expeditious manner.

A lender has occasionally contacted me to say the call with the employer didn't go well. In those cases, I had to call the company's human resources department myself, or get someone else on the line to help. This has a tendency to snowball into negative situations.

The client might be upset because their employer diminished their chances of getting the mortgage or made them look or feel bad in some way. This, of course, gets back to the lender, and the string of events casts a negative light on the entire process.

That's why I like to make everything as clear as possible. If you're redoing your mortgage, for example, we'll need your mortgage statement for all your properties. If there is a rental property involved, we need rental agreements and a property tax bill.

Traditional lenders don't use student income, room rental income, or anything that isn't generally claimed on income taxes. Non-traditional lenders can—and do—use that information, but their interest rate is generally higher to compensate for using alternative information.

If you live in a strata complex, we may require certain strata documents to be ordered prior to an approval. If it's a refinance, restructure, a renewal, or an equity takeout, your lender will require an appraisal as well. Again, the specific situation will determine if the documents are required before or after approval. Keep in mind there's a certain amount of information lenders want upfront and a certain amount they review after receiving the signed commitment.

If there's something unique about your property, let us know in advance. If you took time off for a maternity leave, stress leave, or disability, tell us. If you had a change in your business, you moved locations, or switched from subcontractor to partner, we need to know. If there is a huge construction tarp over your building or a big assessment coming up, give us that information. Don't hide information thinking that it won't come to light. Help us connect the dots. If you can assist us, then of course we can move together to find you a solution. This includes—but is not limited to—a criminal record, previous credit counselling, previous bankruptcy, what Google shows about you, and whether your name is on another title anywhere. Let's get in front of it together to see if we can help.

When that happens, most times we side with our client. But it's not our money, and we don't have the final decision, and we have to work within all the different compliance guidelines.

CHAPTER SEVEN

WHAT TO EXPECT WHEN YOU WORK WITH ME

This section provides an overview of the four steps of my company's unique mortgage process, to illustrate why you are in the best hands with my team or with a mortgage team of my calibre. Everything we do is tailored to result in the most clarity and assistance with your mortgage.

STEP ONE—LET'S TALK!

As mentioned before, once we have your initial information in hand, we get together for an introductory conversation. This is when we see a quick snapshot of what you hope to accomplish. I ask that you come to me with a summary of your scenario with major points (such as learning about buying your first home, your mortgage is coming up for renewal and you are in a certain life stage, or perhaps you have a pending marital separation) affecting financials.

Of all the steps, this one is typically short on duration and long on critical discussion so we can lay a solid foundation.

STEP TWO—OBTAIN PRELIMINARY DOCUMENTS

We don't meet with anyone until we have all the information and documents we need. We have an internal policy of "no docs, no talk," so timing our first "official" meeting depends on the arrival of that information. It isn't efficient to talk about hypothetical situations based on looking at two years of tax returns. Once we have the required information organized and ready to go, we'll let you know. From this point, we can diagnose your situation and move forward.

We can also offer to liaise between you and your advisors should it be needed to initiate the process. Email your accountant, introduce us, and instruct him or her to give us whatever documents we request, the documents that give us exactly what we need on our end. If you're having a difficult time with your strata company trying to figure out what documents you need, we can complete the form for you and then give it to you to submit. When your file is complete, we send everything we have on your file to your lawyer, so that person at least knows what to expect, has your contact information, and knows what lender instructions are coming.

We follow up with the lender every forty-eight hours. They might be waiting for a signature or an approval; there might be a holdup, even a delay over a holiday. These are all things contributing to how quickly we can get your loan completed. Everyone on our team is responsible for certain categories of the process and our goal is to save you as much money as possible before your next mortgage payment.

Timing depends on a number of factors: your application and background, the complexity of the approval, and various lender processes. We can generally turn things around in forty-eight business hours, but that timeline also hinges on how busy the lender is, if the approval is complicated, and how many signatures will be required. Some approvals can be turned around in four hours; others take four days or even four weeks. However, you can rest assured that we ask lenders for an update every forty-eight hours and update you accordingly. Our goal and policy are to complete your file as quickly as possible. Sure, things can come up to affect timing, and we'll address those issues as they arise. Maybe the appraiser couldn't reach you, the house had to be cleaned before sale, the lawyers couldn't fit in that time period, or the underwriter is on vacation.

If it's beneficial to wait to get a more favourable response, that's the route we'll take. If there's a penalty reduction if you wait until your anniversary date, it's better to hold closing until then. If we're waiting for your next pay stub that will reflect the big raise you just received, that can help you qualify for a better mortgage. There are many factors involved and we analyze them on a case-by-case basis.

The documents you need to secure a mortgage are very specific. People sometimes try and send "alternate" documents that don't meet compliance, and we can't move those documents along. If a document is altered, for example, I know delays or possible refusal will come of it. It's best if we follow what works.

Wouldn't you rather provide the correct information initially, instead of scrambling to reach your accountant two days before closing? We follow this protocol based on years of experience. If you choose not to follow it, it will either result in a bad experience for everyone or leave you without the mortgage you want.

REQUIRED DOCUMENTS AND CREDIT SCORES

Let's first discuss the documents you will need. Some of these are required immediately and some later.

If you're using your home equity, or buying your first home, we need three months of account history to back up the origin of the down payment. We'll need a mortgage statement and a home insurance policy. And we need a mortgage application, of course, which takes about five minutes to fill out, including basic information like where you live, your occupation, income, and debts. All of those are pretty clear.

Credit check authorization and credit score are more complicated, but critical to the process. Credit reports have a lot to do with the type of mortgage you are offered; there are different rates available depending on your credit score.

Credit scores of over 700, with at least two trade lines (reports to a credit bureau) in two years will generally get the best options. Anything below 700 can still get a good option, but not the best. Anything below 640—and, of course, anything in the 500s or lower—might be an alternative-lender situation, depending on the basis of the credit. That means we look at the history of how the bills have been paid. Have they been late? How many bills do you have? Was it a one-time circumstance? You also cannot be at your credit limit and receive a high score.

Keep in mind that credit should not extend beyond 80 percent of the available limit, so if the limit on your credit card is $1,000, don't go above $800. Is there anything on your credit report that you already know isn't good or that might reflect poorly on you? It's important for you to discuss these details with us upfront.

If we see something you can do to enhance your credit, we'll verify whatever it is together before submitting. It could be simply a matter of paying off certain loans or paying down credit cards, getting another credit card, or removing information from your credit report that shouldn't be there or that is old or inaccurate. We'll work together over the time period required to get the credit to where we need it.

It doesn't necessarily take much to fix your credit. We had a client whose credit scores didn't reflect her situation accurately. She had paid down some major loans, and so the score should have been better than it was; but one of her credit cards was at the limit and the other one close to it. We knew that once those balances were paid down, her credit score would increase and she could obtain a more favourable mortgage. Once loans are paid down below their balance, credit scores run up. The credit score, combined with timing, reflection of accurate financials, and the anniversary of the mortgage were contributing factors to getting her those benefits.

In some cases, there isn't enough time to change your credit score to get the mortgage you need for your specific circumstances, and that happens. We'll be working alongside you to enhance and improve your scores so we can move your application along to the best available lenders.

HOW TO REHAB A BAD CREDIT SCORE

Your credit score can be deceiving. You might have a score in the 500s but with just one thing screwing it up. Sometimes one or two minor obstacles compound to hurt your score and spiral it to become an inaccurate reflection of your current scenario. Investigating the source often reveals an easy fix; that's why we review everything in detail. Many companies offer credit consulting for a sizable fee, but this service is an integral part of what we do. We don't just tell you the result and what is available. We also formulate a strategy and plan to navigate through murky lending waters.

Even a great credit score doesn't give you a guarantee. We had a client with a 700-plus credit score, but the lender still required a cosigner. It was newer credit, and there wasn't enough active credit on the report. There were only two transaction periods, so it hadn't been established long enough, and there weren't enough details. Because of this, the lender asked for a cosigner.

All lenders are different, but if there's a tricky issue or less-than-desirable credit score, we can guide clients through rebuilding and assist in securing a better mortgage. It doesn't matter what the score is; there's always something that can be done. Unless your credit score is already perfect, the policy for you to work toward is the rule of two: two trade lines, 20 percent below the balances, two years.

What do you do if your credit isn't in great shape and you're having trouble improving your mortgage? Maybe you secured a great mortgage back when your credit shone, but since then your score went down and now you just can't get ahead of it. One thing we can do is keep your first mortgage just the way it is now and get you a second mortgage that allows you to pay out all your debts and improve your credit score. In a few years' time, you can then redo your home mortgage to include everything at once.

Whatever the circumstances, whatever results in the best for you is always what we will recommend, whether that means redoing the whole mortgage or putting together a small second mortgage. This is all part of our short-, mid-, and long-term strategies.

INSURANCE AUTHORIZATIONS

You're going to need insurance—typically, more than one type, including life, disability, and home insurance. It's a condition of funding a mortgage for you to review and accept or decline life and disability insurance, and that you have adequate home insurance to protect your investment. That authorization is given to us at the same time as your credit authorization so these options can be provided. We aren't insurance agents, but we can show you the options so that you can make solid decisions moving forward.

We are going to look for an opportunity to save you money, so we'll typically review whether any mortgage insurance requirement for the lender has been placed on the property and keep that in mind. If you get life and disability insurance with only that lender, then you are stuck there if anything happens. For example, we did a mortgage for a client who had some health issues and had to keep his mortgage with his existing lender or he wouldn't re-qualify for life insurance.

What you have now might not be the best for you forever, but until you've had it reviewed by a professional insurance agent, we'll work closely with you to find your best option. In my opinion, if you can't afford the life and disability insurance, you can't afford the mortgage. We like our clients to be confident that everything will be taken care of, and since it's a condition of funding, it's one less step for you: we'll act as your liaison and automatically send the information over to them to get the ball rolling.

We know that your mortgage is far from your only concern in life. Why not have it taken care of and make life more comfortable? I always suggest taking the insurance and then dealing with it after the fact; you're better off to be insured than not insured. There are many factors involved and if we cannot put together the right program, we will refer you to people who can. There will likely be life changes down the road, and you'll need to deal with them sooner or later.

With home insurance, however, there's no choice: you have to have it. We can help you decide what's needed and ensure that your insurance agent has all the relevant information.

STEP THREE—REVIEW AVAILABLE OPTIONS AND STRATEGIES

In this third step, we review details of the approval and how it compares to other lenders, weigh different options and benefits, and explain how the process works. It doesn't matter if you already have the best mortgage; we still explain our process and your responsibilities.

Once you sign the documents, we work on completion and your lenders do a more vigorous verification process. The lender will call your employer, for example, and verify all your application details. To this point, they haven't yet reviewed 100 percent of the mortgage details and elements, so they're still doing due diligence.

Anything can come up during this review stage, but we're generally ready for it. This part of the process goes quickly—provided, of course, that everything is in place. Obviously, if there are issues with your documentation, the lender will come back to us for clarification, and if something develops with the strata documents, employer call, or appraisal review, we'll deal with that as it comes along.

Sometimes, this process can be finished within a few days and then your documents are off to your lawyer. If we're still waiting on several documents (because we had enough to get approved but not enough to foresee potential glitches), the documents can then be received over a period of time. Your file's specifics will determine the expediency of this part of the process.

POSITIONING TO LENDERS

Lenders like us. That's the simple truth. Our experience, volume, and spot-on organization set us up so most lenders look at our deals first.

We discussed earlier the potential for errors on credit reports. This can take a lot of time to repair because we rely on Equifax to update records, so we may end up waiting for a letter from them and any other party involved. This is out of our control and is based wholly on their processes. We do, however, guide you through what's happening as best we can.

The employer component can be a big help—or a big snag. Sometimes, employers don't return calls on time, or when they do return the call, it's very late in the process because it's not been assigned a high priority in the employer's world. The problem then is that lenders begin to question if you're actually employed there. We had a client who wanted to buy a house in Calgary prior to starting a new position within the company for which they worked. This took place over the Christmas and New Year's holidays (never a good time to conduct mortgage business) and the employer didn't return the lender's call for an extremely extended time. The employer finally got around to calling, but by then the entire situation was viewed by the lender as sketchy, despite the client having been with the firm for eleven years.

The client kept asking if they should remove their subject. We said no. If you choose to remove your subject, it's at your own risk. In this case, the lender came back and said they were unsure about the client's new position and eventually declined the deal. The client had no idea the employer was wavering that much on this potential new job position. When the lender gets a response like that, they're not going to approve the deal. The client ultimately had to change their plans; they ended up staying with the company, but not moving into the role they'd originally discussed.

The takeaway? When things aren't happening, don't try and force it.

STEP FOUR—PLAN APPROVAL AND MAINTENANCE

A plan isn't approved until the lawyers sign off on it. Lenders, in turn, will not start due diligence until they receive everything signed from the borrower.

And things do happen. The client could be in an accident or end up in the hospital with health issues. We've had situations in which everything was done correctly and then two days prior to funding the employer wavered because the lender wanted a guarantee. Sometimes, there's a work injury or a client decides to retire early and the change in situation wasn't reported early enough.

For us, the work begins when the mortgage is funded. Many people think once they sign the documents, that's it. That's not it. We have an ongoing management system in place to ensure the integrity of the plan. Throughout the first year, we have a thirty-day checkup, a six-month checkup, a checkup after twelve months, and then annually after that. We find the thirty-day point is often too early as people are often still moving or in transition. The six-month reminder is an ideal time to ensure everything is going as planned. Every year, we call, email, and mail reminders to connect with us so we can continue helping clients with their plans.

Part of what we do is monitor the market closely for changes that will affect and/or benefit our clients as a group. Many things can change, and there are only so many adjustments we can make at a time. As an example, you can change your variable rate to a fixed rate at any time with no cost and no fees, but if you have a mortgage and wish to take out more money or break the mortgage, you can only do that once a year.

That is why the yearly call is so important, so we can get in touch and make suggestions around market changes. We offer specific recommendations with very clear directions broken down by lender. Remember, this is a collaborative process. Everyone has to be responsible for themselves, and you're the one who makes the decisions, but we also stay in close touch. We send monthly newsletters, we maintain a Facebook page, and I do a weekly radio show.

That's one of our unique advantages, what I call a proactive mortgage strategy. Every new client represents an ongoing relationship that doesn't end with the signing of papers.

Some mortgage providers tend to be transactional. We'd much rather take care of our existing clients and receive multi-generational referrals from them. That's why, once we help a client, we often go on to help their kids, their aunts and uncles, or their parents.

That's a big part of how we've grown our business; all the other things are there as a result of our passion for consistent growth. If a client hasn't done business elsewhere, then all they know is our stellar service and experience. If they *have* worked elsewhere, this is a totally different experience for them and they realize they don't want the people they care about to make a mistake, go somewhere else, and not get this type of service.

In fact, most people wonder why they'd go anywhere else when they can get it all here. It's a very different scenario from what happens with many lenders. It's unusual to see a customer stay with the same bank branch indefinitely. If they see a great new rate and cash-back offer on a window sign, they'll often check it out and consider moving their business.

The goals are just different. We would never advertise that way. When you come to us, you know that you're always going to get the best. If there's a product offering, we offer it to our existing clients, not as a dramatic display to people walking or driving by.

CHAPTER EIGHT

NAVIGATING THE MARKET

One of the things that gives me the most pleasure is sharing my expertise with a wide range of people. Committees, lending institutions, insurers, and the media all seek my opinion. My presence on and participation in these committees is particularly useful, as it allows me to pass on information or considerations to our clients when appropriate. A strong media presence, a place on the front lines of the industry, and an extremely effective execution strategy all allow me to recognize opportunity and execute a proactive strategy for my clients.

When there's a market shift, the first thing we do is identify which clients might be vulnerable. Who will this change impact, and how can I help them get in front of it? In 2008, when the market shifted and rates dropped 50 percent overnight, I immediately recognized an opportunity for my clients and let them know it was time to redo the mortgage before their mortgage anniversaries. There have been a dozen policy changes and opportunities available for our clients since 2008, and every time there's a 0.5 percent shift in the market, either up or down, that's our trigger to review the opportunity and advise clients on exactly what they need to do to optimize that opportunity.

That's a great testament, of course, to client satisfaction. Had they been working with a lender the story would have unfolded very differently. Lenders don't call and say, "I found a way to save you tens of thousands of dollars." It's just not how they operate. We take care of our existing clients first and look to grow organically with more of a family atmosphere. Once a client is a client, they are a part of our tribe, a part of our family.

A large part of this family relationship of market and clients comes from daily monitoring of market fundamentals. I constantly track metrics such as the Canadian dollar, oil prices, employment trends, bond rates, and Bank of Canada activity; stellar independent mortgage professionals in the United States will track similar metrics. Remember that those are the metrics that we track now; as market fundamentals change, the metrics may, too.

Most recently, we saw a lot of regulatory changes affecting people's ability to purchase desired properties as well as their ability to access equity upon renewal. We saw this coming before it became policy. We broke the news in July, and policy went into effect in October. We knew which of our clients would be impacted, immediately sent out appropriate communication, and implemented planning sessions and proactive protection strategies.

THIS ISN'T MY FIRST RODEO

I have enough experience that I don't run around like Chicken Little, warning that the sky is falling. I *do* pay attention to market cues for my clients' benefit. The pendulum swings both ways and we are the best at adapting to formulate the most up-to-date strategies. For example, if a client mentions a need to access more of their equity, and I see opportunities to that effect, they are the first people I call. It's simply a matter of having effective and efficient systems in place to communicate and ensure we're always on top of it. Five years from now, the fundamentals of always watching for the different patterns will be the same—the key is to partner with a team that knows how to execute on the metrics.

One thing we've gotten used to is the yearly cycle of policy changes. Market drivers float out new policies every summer, mostly so there's less public pushback. It's no surprise, then, that we see big market changes in the fall, when the policies take effect.

Change in the mortgage market happens in a heartbeat. Changes can even include which lenders we can access. Lenders are routinely bought and sold. They can change their policies and their process of raising funds. They can be victims of government meddling. There is a plethora of factors involved in our day-to-day business. Unless it's your number-one focus and you're on the front lines, it is nearly impossible to keep up. Even for pros, surprises can happen.

CLARITY BREEDS RELATIONSHIPS

I continue to stress the value of long-term relationships, as they're such a big part of our business. In spite of surprises in the market and unexpected crises, our core values remain the same. Availability and timing of products will vary, as will personal circumstances such as health, employment, credit, or marital status. All of this plays a role in selecting the best product for you.

To make it all come together, open communication is critical, but I have a secret weapon—clarity. There's a reason I earned the 2009 Accredited Mortgage Professional of the Year award. At that time, we'd experienced impressive growth in business during what was a very quiet time in the industry. Framing the mechanics of economics to benefit consumers comes as second nature to me, and I pass that clarity along to my clients.

I think clients come to me because they want the best and because they are open-minded. On our end, those are the clients we want to attract. If someone thinks they know everything about mortgages, they won't come to me. But if someone is of a collaborative mind, understands our core values, and wants this type of ongoing relationship with their mortgage professional, they choose us. If I tell a client that such-and-such a thing is best for them, and it's a strategy that's based on facts and one, moreover, I use on my personal mortgage, should their qualifications allow, they'll follow through. I also have to give credit to smart clients, those who trusted me to help them in the first place.

Even during the financial meltdown, many investment advisors had record years for their clients. They focused on the fundamentals, and they knew where in the market to look to get the right returns. I found that when it was done correctly, it was even worthwhile to pay an occasional penalty. If the penalty was too steep, that was an evaluation we did together, and then it was a matter of knowing the right time to act.

It was a lot like life: part expert wisdom and experience, part crystal ball, and part luck.

We can tie this all together by recognizing it as a mindset of when you are with the right people, you don't have to worry so much about things. We are here to help you throughout the various changes in life, whether personal or with market circumstances, and there is a level of trust built as a result. Our clients understand that when we suggest something, we do so because we care about what's best for them.

THE MARKET IS ITS OWN ANIMAL

I absolutely respect the market; the market is its own animal. You can't tame it. You challenge each other, take wins when you can, and back off before you get trampled.

I can't control the market, government regulation, or economic factors. I can watch fundamentals, but I first need to know what they are. The formula to calculate interest rates can change overnight. I work with existing economic clues and I am as good as the information that's out there. My expertise is the ability to analyze a situation and execute a strategy in a very short time compared to other brokers.

While expertise is invaluable, we still have to be flexible in preparing for what is yet to come. Unpredictable events are always unfolding—wildfires, hurricanes, the housing crisis, or other unforeseen circumstances.

In particular there was the crash of the Chinese stock

market of 2015-2017 that created an absolute real estate frenzy here in Vancouver and Toronto. People wondered why Vancouver real estate flared up as dramatically as it did subsequent to the crash. As soon as the Chinese stock market crashed, everybody with money wanted to diversify as quickly as possible, and by the world's standards, Canada had some relatively cheap real estate. Buyers flooded the market, buying property at any price. They would literally outbid any regional buyer, making it impossible to compete. If a seller is considering two offers and one is, "Write your own cheque. Whatever you want us to pay, we'll pay it," and the other says, "I need subject to financing and I need an inspection," which are they going to choose?

In April of 2018, we saw a fifty-basis-point jump in the bond market. We know that whenever the bond market goes up, it affects interest rates. For our clients with pre-approvals nearing expiration, and those waiting to renew or lock in an option, this could be important. We let them know three weeks before the jump. Every month, we look at all of our clients to see who can benefit and make changes accordingly. We then look at "pre-clients," people who have something in the works. Then we go to the general public. If you're in our system, you're in our family, and we take care of our own.

Sometimes, you don't see a pattern right away, and before

you know it, an entire market shifts before your eyes. We might not be able to connect the dots at first, but we *can* over time, and that ability arms us with experience and knowledge on hand for future scenarios. The truth is that there is too much in the world that's completely out of our control. Any economist, any financial advisor who says that they can predict more than a few months out just isn't being honest. No one can. And that's upsetting to people. We want to know, we want to be in control, and sometimes when someone offers us the illusion of control we reach out for it eagerly. Life feels complicated enough.

I understand that feeling, but it's an emotional reaction, not a thoughtful one. We don't make promises that we can't fulfill, because we can't predict beyond a certain time frame. We can look at patterns of what's happened in the past and make intelligent guesses about the future from them; we can look at what's currently shifting and what economic indicators tell us might shift some more; and we can promise to act immediately once we have accurate information in hand. We're committed to doing the best that we can within a given set of circumstances.

This reinforces the concept that it pays to hire an expert focused on the task at hand. Someone intimately familiar with the industry's daily workings—and how they change— can help you make the best decisions for your situation. Just like a medical general practitioner, we understand the big picture related to your financial health, but our focus is to help you with one area: mortgages.

Financial advisors can play a big role in your life, but their primary role is to advise you on how to make specific investments in certain stocks and funds compatible with your goals. In my experience, people often make the mistake of believing that a financial advisor will also understand how to give the best mortgage advice, but they're already spread thin in their position. I'm not a licensed financial advisor, but I do have general understanding and much investment experience. I know my role and I do it well.

UNDERSTANDING AND OPTIMIZING THE MARKET

Since the drastic market shift of 2008, there have been at least a dozen policy changes and opportunities available for our clients. Every time there is a 0.5 percent market shift, up or down, it's our trigger to review potential new opportunities.

Here's an example of one of those opportunities. I met a young couple some time ago. They held jobs, respectively, as a mechanic and office administrator, and had recently purchased their first home. They bought it at a 5.99 percent interest rate, a 5 percent down payment, and a forty-year mortgage. We recognized an opportunity within the market to redo their mortgage at 3.79 percent and, even after the prepayment penalty, we were able to cut their payments in half and reduce their amortization. It changed their lives completely.

They were people with simple needs, newly married, and expecting their first baby. They didn't have plans to buy investment properties or to have more children. They only wanted to live a wholesome life in a comfortable home. They initially thought the new mom would have to go back to work after the baby arrived but, as a result of our strategy, they were able to build a secondary suite in their house and have the mother-in-law stay with them. Today, the couple is moving into their early forties and they're going to be mortgage-free very soon, with the quality of life they wanted, while now being open to other opportunities to build their wealth accordingly.

There are many different circumstances like this, and the moral of the story is that good advice works. It's harder and harder to make ends meet in both Canada and the United States, with wages not increasing as fast as the cost of living. We're also seeing a dramatic gender and age demographic change. It's become common for older, retired people to *have* to go back to work, and we've helped a lot of clients who thought their retired life would mean not working anymore so they could enjoy the quality of life they'd earned after decades of hard work. Because of our ongoing mortgage management and opportunities in the market, we've often been able to redo mortgages to allow them to enjoy a better quality of life. For some people, quality of life means owning ten properties. For others, it means just being able to live a simple life.

Whatever your goal is, for me it's a pleasure to see you enjoy whatever you're looking for. I am personally passionate about real estate and investing. For me, success is about growth and opportunities, investments and excitement. I'm able to share that with like-minded clients and it is terrifically rewarding. By the same token, many of my best friends live simple, fulfilling lives thanks to solid financial advice. Success means different things to everyone.

Maybe it means not having to work overtime. Maybe it means going to your kid's soccer game. Maybe it means a mom doesn't have to go stock shelves all night at the local market just to provide for her kids.

I take great pride in helping people live full lives. I strive to be the best person I can be and contribute however I can to give back to others.

A MORTGAGE SWITCH IN THE NICK OF TIME

I'll never forget a last-minute equity deal we made for one

Langley couple, Helen and David. They were closing in on retirement, and certain policies were about to change that would allow them less access to their money. They'd planned to use the money for investments, vacationing, and general life events.

We immediately sent emails to tell them the change was coming up. "If you ever considered accessing your equity," I wrote, "or if we want to look at changing your mortgage a little earlier than we anticipated, now's the time for us to do it." We knew about the legislation changes in July, well in advance of implementation, and the advance notice allowed our clients three months to prepare. Other brokers and clients asked how we kept up with the influx of projects in market changes like this, but we didn't see it as a drastic change: we knew the change was coming and continued to serve our clients through our usual processes. We execute according to market shifts and client scenarios to provide the most valuable benefits.

To me, the biggest advantage to working with us is our proactivity. We want our borrowers to be as educated as possible. Once you have a mortgage from a bank, it's most common that the only time you're going to hear from them is if their call centre contacts you with a sales opportunity. We'll be contacting you every time we find a way to improve your life.

MARITAL CHANGES AND PROPERTY SHIFTS

Changes in marital status often create sticky financial situations and people often panic. They don't need to, because for us this is just business as usual, a challenge to face and a solution to find.

I'm thinking of one couple in particular. When we had helped these clients originally, they were married. One of them worked as an engineer, the other was on the board of a local charity. They'd had some issues already within their marriage and came to us looking for something more flexible, so if one of them needed to access a large chunk of money, they could do it. They had considered purchasing a rental property—using equity to complete the transaction quickly—but their relationship issues got in the way. Now, instead of buying the rental property, they were deciding to separate.

We helped them take their original goals and modify them successfully. We helped one of the spouses buy out the other without making any changes to the home so they could maintain consistency for the children; we did that by using the money set aside for the rental purchase. The husband subsequently remarried, and his new wife happened to own a rental property. We moved some of that equity so they could combine forces and move up the property ladder together. They just recently welcomed a new addition to their family, too.

But it wasn't completely smooth sailing. The husband and his new wife were living together. He thought it would be beneficial if he owned part of her rental property. We saw a potential money loss with this plan: if he added his name to the title, he would owe property transfer tax. Anyone getting involved in title of property is completely responsible for the implications. They decided in the end that it wasn't worth it for him to go on title just for the sake of estate planning purposes. While we have experience with this within our practice it is important to discuss title changes with a lawyer to confirm what is applicable for you in the preliminary stage of the process.

ORGANIC SOLUTIONS

Another time we helped a gentleman buy a condo. His girlfriend also owned a condo. They eventually bought a home together, keeping their respective condos as rental properties. Fast-forward a few years and they wanted to buy a vacation property in the interior. The only way they qualified to take money out of one of the rentals (for a down payment on the vacation property) was if he went on title for that rental. It would work, but that also meant tax consequences. This time, the benefit outweighed the disadvantage, and the transaction worked out perfectly.

Everyone's situation is different. A single woman was saving money so she and her boyfriend could buy a place together. He already had a condo of his own, though, and was dragging his feet on consolidating their living situations. I eventually advised her to stop waiting and buy her own place; she was losing time she could be earning equity on the market. She eventually bought a place that she considered renting out. Again, I was able to help her save money: I urged her to wait at least a year or she'd have to pay back the first-time homebuyer advantage she'd received in the first place.

As you can see, all these situations end up being an organic mix of financial and relationship guidance, because engaging in every aspect of a client's life makes the financial piece fit in naturally and perfectly. It's very rewarding, especially when we see a happy ending.

CAUTIONARY TALES

We have an outstanding record of victories for clients, but things aren't rosy every time. We must always be cautious and prepared for the unexpected.

Anthony is a self-employed client, and the lender wasn't quite happy with his credit. Anthony had his eye on a house, and the lender said they would review this deal only with a strong cosigner. Anthony's dad is a doctor, and of course said he would sign on. But there was a catch: Anthony has a brother and a sister. I wanted to be sure

Anthony and his dad knew that even though his father was only a "guarantor," he was still responsible for that mortgage. Dad made great money, but this new house wasn't his principal residence. He obviously didn't want to pay tax on that and being tied to another residence would block him from qualifying for a larger home, or from helping out his other children in similar circumstances. We worked out a creative solution that benefitted everyone: a gift option. Anthony's father gave him 10 percent as a down payment so he didn't have the financial encumbrance down the road. In some cases, parents can go on the mortgage and not on title, but again, as everyone's fingerprints are unique to them, so are the offers and options available at the time of the scenario for the borrower.

This also goes the other way for senior parents. Senior parents on a limited retirement income may not have had the opportunity to understand about being proactive with a mortgage. Their kids might not be able to qualify to cosign for them because maybe the kids themselves need to qualify for a new car or a new house.

COSIGNING CONUNDRUM

When parents or other parties are quick to cosign on a mortgage loan it can create problems. I had a client who didn't make enough money to qualify on her own. Her sister planned to cosign for her, but they weren't familiar with the possible ramifications. Lenders are very quick to suggest a cosigner but very slow to remind the cosigner they are on the hook for every single dollar involved. If something happens down the road—a new relationship, you want to buy a place, you get a new job—your name on that mortgage could mean problems. There's no guarantee as to when you can or cannot get off the mortgage. If, for example, you don't show enough income five years from now, your credit isn't in the best place, or your property value doesn't go up, you might not be able to refinance.

In many past scenarios like this, we've had parents who refinanced their house to give their kids down payments instead of cosigning. This is called "gifting equity," and it has proven to give a much better result: it's as clean as possible and protects everyone. Sometimes pulling investments to gift or lend money to a loved one can come with tax implications that always should be reviewed with your financial advisor, accountant, and lawyer.

MORTGAGE PAYMENT MALFUNCTION

We had a client, a software developer, who was a high-income earner. He wanted to make a $50,000 lump sum payment on his mortgage. That can be a great idea, but it's critical to consider all the angles.

The company he works for doesn't have a pension plan.

I asked him if he was sure about making the lump sum payment, in light of those circumstances. "Have you considered making that contribution to an RRSP so you can reduce the amount of income tax you pay?" I asked. "If it brings you into the next tax bracket, it can potentially give you a refund you can put down on your mortgage, and you'll also have saved for retirement."

He hadn't even considered this option. I asked if he'd contributed to his children's Registered Education Savings Plans. In Canada, there's an incentive in place allowing you to contribute to an RESP, and the government will match part of the amount, essentially giving you free money for education expenses. If your kids don't go to school, then you pay back the amount, but you still get to keep the dividends earned from the investment.

It's so important to look at the whole picture. I asked him, "Do you have six months of living expenses set aside?" He did not. "Okay, priority number one should be having six months of living expenses on hand. Priority number two should be looking at everything else to ensure you've maximized it for your opportunities, like putting money into RESPs or future property investment or a move up the ladder that you would need to have a deposit ready in hand with."

I urged him not to be too quick to put all that money into

his mortgage. It wouldn't benefit him or reduce his payments, aside from shrinking the amount he owed at the end of the term. We had to think strategically on the best place for that money. Paying down your mortgage is great—when everything else has been considered.

WHEN YOU'RE IN IT TOGETHER

It's no secret that relationships require commitment and hard work. It's also common to see many relationships fail. Financial responsibilities bring another level of problems but staying smart and planning ahead helps smooth the waters.

I had clients, a couple in the process of separating, and they were looking at buying a house as an investment and a potential home for their children. They knew it wasn't wise for both of them to throw money away on rent. We looked closely at the scenario and made sure we had a mortgage best suited for them that they could exit, if need be, at the lowest cost. This was a situation that considered not only market opportunities, but personal components as well.

If this couple had approached a lender directly, their scenario could have negatively affected their qualifications and likelihood of approval; because each lender has a bias, they wouldn't have known if this was the best path forward. This is another example of the way we genuinely care for our clients' needs and help them move forward. Anytime you go to a lender on your own, you pay the price for not necessarily getting the best advice.

MOVING UP THE PROPERTY LADDER

CHAPTER NINE

REVIEWING AN EXISTING MORTGAGE

Securing an ideally structured mortgage is an admirable step, but don't stop there. It's important to review mortgage details on a regular basis. The review doesn't cost anything, and clients should remember it is a time investment to ensure they're doing what's best for their future.

As we've seen, once you're a client, we review your mortgage yearly. If you're reading this book and you don't have a mortgage with us, or it's been a year since you renegotiated your existing mortgage, email us right now. Let's get to work, learn about you and your scenario, and see what we can do to help you.

As part of the review, we check on personal circumstances, market changes, insurance metrics, and policy shifts.

Mortgages are very complex, and I don't feel anybody is aware enough to handle it all unless they've been on the front lines of the industry. Depending on when and how the mortgage was underwritten, it will come with certain policies and opportunities from which you might benefit. There are different sets of rules, interest rates, and products available depending on the state of your mortgage (insured or uninsured) and your particular circumstances. We evaluate all that before making any recommendations.

Most people think they can't afford an investment property, and only apply for mortgages for a primary residence. But if you're reviewing your mortgage regularly and planning early for retirement, an investment property might end up being an excellent fit, both for you and for your family.

One of my girlfriends is an ideal example of staying mortgage-smart. She knows I buy real estate as frequently as possible. She also knows I bought properties when my children were born that I intend will be theirs one day. She and her husband, both high-income earners, have a thirteen-year-old son planning to attend Simon Fraser University in Burnaby. She wanted to take advantage of property market appreciation and buy something to rent out. She bought a presale that will be completed in about a year, so she'll have appreciation in the market. She can rent it out until her son is of age, and he can live there while he's at university.

It's never too soon to buy property. I had a client who was literally living in his parents' basement, but he bought a presale for $400,000. Three years later, it was worth $1.2 million (most of us won't see that kind of return, of course!). His parents gave him early inheritance money for the deposit and he was able to live under their roof and save more money to put down on his soon to be home. After he lives in it a year, he'll be able to refinance and pay his parents back, even though it was a gift that wasn't required to be paid back. He wanted to thank them for their teamwork in helping him achieve his goal. The whole scenario allowed the client to get a property he wanted while his parents earned a solid investment.

People often come to me for this type of planning because they know I'm doing it myself. I had a dentist client who lived right around the corner from me. She wanted to buy her "downsized house" so she could have the best of both worlds. She wanted a rental property right now to generate revenue and also secure something she'd like to live in when she retires. She purchased the house and it's bringing her revenue and extra monthly income. Best of all, both properties are appreciating in value.

Why wait to downsize if you can access your equity early, get someone else paying that mortgage, and enjoy the appreciation in the meantime? This seems like simple advice, but many people don't think to act on it until they see other people doing something similar. A lot of it is simply learning how to use your money as intelligently as possible to make for a much better life. The best answers are usually the simplest, but you often don't see them until someone points them out.

It's like staring at a puddle and wondering how you're going to get over it without getting wet, and someone comes along and jumps right over it. You suddenly realize you, too, could have jumped over it. You can jump or walk around the puddle as well as the next person; sometimes, you just need to see it in action to spark the confidence to take the step.

It's essential to reinforce what we noted earlier about having your own real estate expert. When you're on the journey of purchasing a presale or an existing residence, selling yours, buying a rental, or bidding on a foreclosure, these experts advocate for you. They'll get you the necessary documents, answer the questions lenders will ask about a property, get you in to preview properties in advance, chase down the seller's agent to encourage them to meet the tight timelines for inspections appraisal, and answer questions that come up through the hundreds of papers reviewed to help you with clarity on exactly what you are buying.

It's essential to do this with someone who doesn't have

a bias related to the property you are buying. Good real estate agents know that things change—no matter how long they've been in the business or how many transactions they've done. If a lender is asking for something, it's because they need it. You need to engage with professionals who don't waste precious time on why something is needed or why it wasn't requested before. They know there's a reason and strategy behind everything asked for and the time in the process it's asked for. Real estate agents and mortgage professionals have to see themselves as part of a team: the team that can make things happen for you.

WHAT TO EXPECT WHEN REFINANCING

As we've seen, the fundamentals of any mortgage exploration include a brief consultation, gathering of documents, conditional approval, and then "file complete." Much of the process of refinancing follows the same course as we normally follow for any mortgage.

When you refinance, you change the structure of the mortgage, so you have a lot of flexibility. You will generally change the amortization, the title, or the people on the title, but we additionally keep an eye out for anything that may benefit you. It could be an entirely new mortgage, a wait term, or a short-term cleanup to get us where we want to go.

When a straight renewal comes along, we obviously look at your existing scenario, and if we believe you're best suited to your existing lender, we'll recommend you stay put. If there's a better option, we'll steer you in that direction. But the process is the same every time. We evaluate what we have and stay proactive with what we need.

Depending on the scenario, an appraisal of the property might be required. We recommend getting an appraisal upfront in certain situations. Last-minute details can come up that we don't expect; if that happens, we'll meet to review the approval process. If necessary, we can change the direction or narrative of our strategy.

We have a tried-and-true system with years of proven results. If clients follow the process, it will be smooth sailing from start to finish. In-person meetings, for example, are enormously helpful, providing all parties are present to receive the information. If only one person shows up, they have to take the information home to discuss with their partner or family, and things can easily get lost in translation. It's not an effective or efficient way to help our clients and in many cases it leads to frustration.

RENEWALS

When your mortgage comes up for renewal (this happens in Canada, but not in the United States), you could end up with a higher payment than anticipated, even if your balance is lower. It's easy for people to forget or lose track of fluctuating interest rates. You must be very careful with renewals, because this is often where lenders try to sneak things in, and you might end up receiving different terms than you expected.

Some of the lenders we work with will actually send their renewals to us to review, because they get the bulk of their business from brokers. In those cases, unless you're getting any new money, or there's been a significant shift in your scenario, we recommend you sign with them. That's why we go through the same process at renewal we went through when we initially secured your mortgage, because we remain alert and available throughout the process.

If the bond market jumps fifty points, for example, you need to adjust your mortgage payment now to avoid future payment shock. Remember if you increase your payments, even if your particular rate is not increasing, you still reap the benefits of paying off the mortgage faster and with less interest.

We always want to ensure you know we've all been in touch with each other and we're going to review the information together to make sure it's the best fit for you. Provided our clients get approved with one of the best monoline lenders in Canada, nine times out of ten my team is just involved in helping renew the mortgage with that lender. Of course, if lenders need to make a change for some reason, or they want access to more money because the renewals are better than what they're offering their new clients, we will meet to discuss your options.

THE FORECLOSURE ADVENTURE

Buying a foreclosure property isn't a typical real estate transaction. You must prepare for a different process and financial worst-case scenario. I want to be very clear: if you're buying a foreclosure, you have to determine first if you have the guts to do what you need to do. If you don't and you're not willing to put your money where your mouth is, a foreclosure is not for you. When you buy a foreclosure, prepare to spend money on an appraisal upfront (generally between $300 and $400) and know you might need two appraisals: one to determine what you're comfortable paying, and another for your lender, the latter depending on the closing date and the lender's policies.

Keep in mind that just because you're willing to pay a certain amount for a property doesn't mean the lender will lend that amount on what they believe the value to be. If there's any difference between those amounts, as the customer, you must be prepared to pay for it.

With foreclosures, one of the most important factors to

consider is the status of the property. The lender might insist on certain wiring, or that the property be brought up to a specific condition with which they are comfortable. Sometimes foreclosures are done in the middle of a renovation, and the lender will require the work to be 97 to 99 percent complete, with the proper occupancy permit, before they'll lend on it. In these cases, you either have to have the money to do those renovations or be willing to take a "purchase plus improvements" mortgage, in which you pay the money upfront and then the lender pays back the contractors when the work is completed.

You pay interest on the money from day one, but you don't get the money from the mortgage until after work on the property is finished, which can come with its own set of problems. It can be a good thing, but you have to take an informed approach.

In other scenarios, an appraiser might say, "We only believe the economic life of this property to be twenty years, therefore we're only going to give you a mortgage for fifteen years." And that's assuming you even qualify for it in the first place, because now your payments will be higher.

Many people don't want to spend that kind of money, and most lenders won't give an approval until an offer is accepted, clear of any potential problems. The lender has the right to modify their approval at any time based on their audit. If anything changes, the buyer is the one responsible.

Properties in foreclosure are typically foreclosed upon because the owners can't afford to make their payments, so when you go to bid on a property, there are generally a lot of emotions in play. People tend to outbid each other because they want the property, but often you will have to buy "as is, where is."

Foreclosures aren't the easiest financing in the world. We'll get you the mortgage we can, but you have to be clear that with anything happening after the fact, it is what it is! It's crucial that you stay flexible, have your documents in order, and prepare yourself for the unexpected. It's a buyer-beware situation. In one instance, the lender initially didn't even want an appraisal because it was an insured mortgage. Five days before completion they decided they wanted an appraisal. We had to get the appraisal, and they cut the amortization down five years, even after they had already signed off on it.

With a foreclosure, you don't generally have a choice to walk away from the property, because you won it through bidding. Other properties have a subject period during which you can back out if something comes up or terminate your subjects due to financing or appraisal review from the lender. Not with foreclosures.

In other words, be prepared.

THE PRESALE ROLLERCOASTER

A presale—buying a home before it's been built—is another challenging scenario. As I write this, people who bought presales are vulnerable. January of 2018 ushered in significant changes in the presale market. If you bought a presale in 2017 and it wasn't to be completed until 2019, the qualification landscape changed, so we need to put a different plan in place for you. If you've qualified based on the old rules, we'll have to look at putting more money down, securing a cosigner, or selling another property.

Presales come with a great upside, however. The market appreciates, and you get a new product at today's price.

The catch is this: lenders don't have to honour their original approval. Someone who approved you a year, six months, six weeks, or six hours ago doesn't have to honour the approval if they see a change in your qualification. Even with new legislative guidelines, there are still lenders that will adapt on the fly: it's how they handle appraised value. Keep in mind that lenders always have the right to modify their approval. For example, eight years ago, anyone with a line of credit instantly had it increased because of variable rate contracts. Now if the mortgage hasn't funded, the lender has the option of breaking the contract. Details are still to be determined, and we'll learn more in the upcoming months and years as to how the changes translate to owners.

When I bought my first home, I was still living in my parents' house, and the truth is I couldn't qualify for the mortgage! I was working as a receptionist, I was in the process of getting licensed as a mortgage broker, and my income wasn't what it needed to be for me to qualify if I had to close on it shortly. The good news was I had three to four years and a few backup plans to count on, so I calculated the risk that I took.

I knew what income I needed to qualify, so I was going to make it happen (like a line from a television character, "things happen 'cause I make them happen"). Living at home, I had time to save more of a down payment, and if this meant I didn't spend a penny until I closed, that's what I would have done.

Another option was my parents either cosigning or refinancing to help me.

If none of those options happened, then I'd lose my deposit, but it was a risk I was willing to take. Even with plans—and backup plans—in place, life stepped in and changes came tumbling down on me anyway. Qualifications for the presale changed, requiring a more substantial down payment. I'd met my future husband (and he lived out in the suburbs near my office). Before I completed on this home, my employment status had changed, and my relationship status had changed. I had to be ready to change on a dime.

I didn't want to move in with my boyfriend for a couple of reasons. He'd already lived in his house with a former girlfriend. Besides, according to my own Italian tradition, you wait until marriage to live together. What did I do? I bought my own house around the corner, of course! It can be a good thing to keep your finances separate from your relationships, and that proved to be the answer for us.

Thankfully, I had a plan in place, it was a calculated risk with backup plans, and I was ready to accept the result of what I had taken on in the event things didn't go the way I wanted them to. I sure was glad I was in this business, and it taught me a lot in terms of how I could share my experiences with others to empower their decisions.

The only person this falls back on is the borrower. I had a client who changed jobs after a presale approval and the lender declined the application, and there was a client whose presale property value dropped so he had to make a more substantial down payment.

We work with the cards we're dealt; we're not the dealer. Remember that when you say, "hit me" in blackjack, the dealer isn't responsible for what happens when the cards turn over!

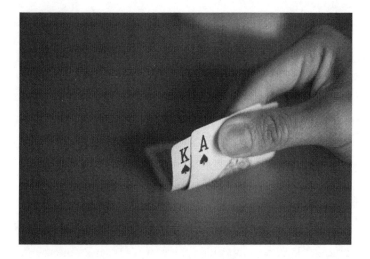

PUT YOUR AMORTIZATION TO WORK

We always recommend you take the longest amortization possible, because the amortization doesn't actually dictate the duration of your mortgage payments; that duration is determined by how you set up your payment. If you have a long amortization, you can always revert back to the minimum payment. This helps you avoid accumulating outside debt, and you can qualify for something else if you need to. If you want to buy a rental, but you've just renewed your principal residence mortgage at fifteen years, you won't qualify. But if you had your principal on a thirty-year term, it would allow much more flexibility.

If we recommend a straight switch, then of course we're not going to recommend the longer amortization, because it's a product-specific circumstance.

There are lenders offering thirty-five-year amortization, but their interest rates are higher, so we don't recommend that option unless it's beneficial for the borrower. Longer amortizations essentially offer built-in free insurance for you. We always try to build a safety net in case something comes up in your life. If it does, you can just stop making extra payments and avoid incurring outside debt.

If you get an appraisal and the property only has thirty years of economic life remaining, some lenders will offer you financing at twenty-five years. Every lender has different policies as to what economic life they need to have remaining for certain amortization, and we may or may not agree with their decision. The only other option is to get another appraisal, but if we feel it might deliver the same result, you have to decide if you can handle the expense. If not, the financing option could be suitable enough.

The takeaway here is we'll always look for the best option for your future with what we can control to empower you.

THE BRIDGE BETWEEN TWO LOANS

Let's talk about bridge loans. Bridge loans are short-term financing on a down payment assisting purchasers to "bridge" the gap between an old and new mortgage. These loans can help you out of sticky situations, with few associated fees, and provide interim financing.

The cost of a bridge loan comprises two parts:

1. The interest rate charged on the amount of funds borrowed. This is based on the prime rate and varies from lender to lender.
2. An administrative fee. Again, this varies between lenders and can range from $200 to $700.

Many people think getting a bridge loan is a simple thing, but it is absolutely not. You need to contact us before you consider selling your home, not when your home is already on the market. Once your home is on the market, there's no guarantee it will be sold. The only way you can get a bridge is with a guaranteed sale date on your house.

Think of it as you would a bridge over a river: you don't want to cross it without knowing where it leads. It's no different with a mortgage. No lender will give you money to hold both mortgages when they can't see the end of the bridge. And they aren't in the speculation business when it comes to bridge financing; you can only qualify for a bridge loan when you've sold a home with a certain sale date and a contract in hand.

When considering timing, keep in mind completion for bridge loans is in the range of thirty to ninety days. Some lenders will go to one hundred twenty days in certain cases. Your bridge amount and duration will dictate if you are required to change lenders from your original plan.

Bridge loans can be helpful and tricky at the same time. I'm not a huge fan of people buying before they sell, because it usually creates the most amount of stress and costs them the most amount of money in the end. They're usually under pressure to sell at a certain price, and obviously have to pay money (which they might or might not have) for bridge financing. Many people think just because they've bought another place and their original house is listed, they somehow qualify for a bridge. That's not true.

Every lender is different in terms of what they accept for a bridge.

Scenarios and implementation for bridge loans are wildly different. Some people register with a lawyer. Some people want promissory notes. Your unique circumstance will determine what your bridge loan will look like.

Remember, you can't get bridge financing from a lender who's not doing the mortgage. We often get calls from people who are downsizing. They are typically used to doing business on a handshake at the local branch and say, "Well, I bought a new place, and I haven't sold my other place yet. Can you give me a bridge?"

If no one is doing a new mortgage, then there's no bridge for you. A lender might approve it as a line of credit—provided you qualify—but it's expensive. The lesson is clear: don't buy before you sell. Before you've listed your property, get everything in place so you don't have to work on anyone else's timeline. If you do things right, and you have enough equity and a clear title, then we can get you a mortgage product that allows you access to your equity without having to pay interest on it until you use it.

It's so much more comfortable doing things on your own timeline. It goes back to the idea of understanding the mortgage code. Don't be a victim of someone else's timing; create your own. You can do it by being proactive. We can help you deploy and execute on that intelligence, but you need to prepare.

Generally, bridge loans increase in volume when the market is really hot. In a hot market, people tend to not do subject-to-sale transactions. Everything is going through in multiple offers and buyers are pressured to put in bids. It all comes down to the cycle of the market in a particular neighbourhood.

THE REVERSE-MORTGAGE TIME MACHINE

Reverse mortgages have come a long way over the years and offer a great option for accessing equity for people who are house-rich and cash-poor. Of course, we hope every client has taken advantage of strategic planning and is financially stable, but a reverse mortgage can often be an excellent solution for people past their working years who are living solely on retirement income. They often cannot qualify for traditional mortgage options, and a reverse helps them get where they need to go. As a bonus, reverse mortgages are typically affordable because they have no monthly payments (payments are taken when the property is sold).

Two of our clients were elderly widows living together in a condo. They'd each lost their husband around the same time, and neither of them wanted to live alone, so the mutual living space worked very well. They'd both gotten married in their early twenties, and now their children were in their fifties. After some time, one of the women fell ill and wanted to live out her remaining days with her son and to provide money for her care moving forward. A few physical changes would have to be made to her son's home and she didn't want to be a financial burden on him. She couldn't afford a traditional mortgage, so she took out a reverse mortgage on the condo property to buy out the other widow—and she even had money left over. The family was happy, received some of their wealth early, and had funds available to provide their mother with the medical care she needed.

A review five and ten years prior to retirement will provide the best plan to access your equity at a later date in the most cost-effective and strategic manner.

PRIVATE MORTGAGES

Related to the reverse mortgage scenario is the private mortgage option, where you keep the terms of your first mortgage but are looking at different criteria. This can sometimes mean higher rates and fees, but in some cases this option makes financial sense.

We had a client couple in a less-than-ideal situation.

When they originally got their mortgage, they were both employed and doing very well. Over the course of five years, the husband started a company that wasn't as successful as they had hoped, and they ended up accumulating a great deal of personal debt. They were audited, they owed back taxes, and his credit score took a hit.

We reviewed the situation and developed a strategy for them. In light of their existing qualifications, it was best to renew their mortgage with their existing lender. Instead of paying a high rate and a high fee on the entire mortgage amount, we secured a private second mortgage for a smaller amount to pay out the taxes and debts owed. Doing so increased the husband's credit score; now, when their mortgage is up for renewal, they'll qualify for a better option. It was better to take the higher rate and fee on the second mortgage, clean everything up, and then renew all of it a couple years down the road.

WHAT YOU NEED TO KNOW ABOUT YOUR HOME EQUITY

A false sense of security surrounds home equity. It's not really your own until it's accessed through a loan. It can fluctuate, and access to it is not always easy.

Understanding equity can be challenging, to be sure. Many people are lulled into complacency, assuming they're fine because they have the home-equity security blanket. The reality is we cannot rely on it and need to approach it intelligently, apply knowledge to what's happening, and remain strategic and methodical.

Having equity is not enough. It's not enough to help you qualify for the best options. You can't assume your equity can speak for itself. On the surface, you would think people with more equity would get better interest rates, but the way the interest rate market works, people with the least amount of equity at times get better interest rates because their mortgages can be insured.

You might be surprised to find out you won't always be able to do what you want to do. A retired person with reduced income interested in buying a property might qualify for less with recent rule changes: there might be increased debt and reduced income, and the strategy might have to change. If you're late to the movies, you might not get the seats you want!

Current Canadian regulations are implementing additional stress tests on mortgages, and many people now qualify for less. The simple truth is the government doesn't want to allow homeowners to use their homes as equity. We're consistently striving to help clients stay ahead of government regulations so they can keep control. I've never seen people with so much equity be so frustrated.

There will always be obstacles to overcome, but working together, we can adapt and stay ahead of changes to maintain a positive outcome.

CHAPTER TEN

BREAKING A MORTGAGE EARLY

As you've probably understood by now, there are no guarantees with mortgages. Planning is critical to understanding mortgage terms and how they apply to your situation. We'll help by working collaboratively and acting on suitable recommendations at the right time. Mortgage policies change rapidly and you might not qualify today for something you qualified for yesterday. And the same is true for breaking mortgages as well.

There's a collection of common scenarios around breaking a mortgage early, the most common being relationship status. If you're recently married or divorced (or in flux between the two), you might have occasion to break your mortgage. Adding children, or having children leave the household, also has a big effect on a mortgage. Health, income, neighbourhood rezoning, and even moving simply because you don't like your neighbours are also themes we see frequently.

All of the above scenarios are important, but I think the most important thing for everyone to know is how to use their equity most efficiently. When you own a home and contribute to it on a monthly basis, yet you have additional debts of $10,000 or more, it's time to see if you qualify to include those debts in your mortgage. This is typically the most cost-effective strategy for most people. If for whatever reason your mortgage professional thinks another avenue besides a mortgage will be more financially beneficial, they'll let you know.

Debt is still debt. Even if you have a car loan at 0 percent, it's still costing you between $600 and $800 a month. You might have a cash outflow that's taking away opportunities to qualify for a mortgage upwards of $2,000 to $3,000. If being able to get credit in the future and gaining better cash flow is important to you, you can break the cycle of debt so common in Canada today.

These days, wages aren't keeping up with inflation because labour is sourced to other countries for much less than it costs here in North America. Knowing we don't make as much money as we used to, we have to look at our debt intelligently and at how we can improve our personal cash flow to best enhance our own financial balance.

My focus here, and the focus of this book, is moving credit-card debt, lines of credit, vehicle debt, and other expenses inside your mortgage where the interest rate will be lower and amortized over a reasonable period of time. This provides the best cash flow. We understand that life happens. You buy a house and then your car breaks down. You planned on having two kids, but then you end up having three, and now you need a seven-seater vehicle. The list is long.

More often than not, debt burden is a result of the society in which we live. If you can ask yourself these three questions and the answer is no, then reviewing a refinance opportunity is in your best interests:

- Are you receiving a significant bonus from your job in the next ninety days?
- Will you receive proceeds from sale of an asset in the next ninety days?
- Are you receiving proceeds from an inheritance?

We are currently seeing a significant transition of wealth from people who have retired, and—believe it or not—a large percentage of Canadians don't actually have mortgages on their homes. When they pass away and transfer the estate to their families, the transfer of wealth will be reinvested in our society through multiple generations.

Of course, not everybody will be in a position to refinance. For some people, the penalty could be too punitive and not allow refinancing. This is another point where I'd like to reinforce, when we have the opportunity—because the client qualifies accordingly based on their life stage, income and credit, timing, and property—we look to first place their mortgage with a monoline lender.

Business accounts differ, of course, and you still must be aware of anomalies. We have had accountants explain that in Canada the business write-off for a vehicle can be up to $800 a month. It doesn't matter. If you cannot afford the monthly payments due to employee wages, cost of goods, or what have you, it makes sense to consolidate those payments into a mortgage. There are always financial distractions to navigate.

Understanding that a higher percentage rate at times is most cost-effective or might be more beneficial, depending on circumstances, shows that you are better positioned for working with a mortgage professional. This aspect of mortgage planning is critical, because understanding it can save you money and help you move up the property ladder.

We can't count on mortgage rates and plans to remain the same forever, any more than we can predict anything that happens in life. And it's precisely the uncertainties of the future that are important in mortgage planning. Can you guarantee you will never get divorced, your job will always be secure, or the market will stay the same and you'll never need equity from your home?

DIVORCE

One of the major reasons people break mortgages early is divorce, so it's worthwhile taking a moment to think about divorce implications in mortgages.

Since most couples have a joint mortgage—one in which both names are on the mortgage and title of the home—when separation or divorce proceedings get underway, most people wonder what will happen with their home.

When the marriage comes to an end, there are two obvious options concerning the home:

- Sell the property and split the proceeds according to your agreement and go your separate ways
- One person buys the other party out of the mortgage and the title of the property

The first option is a straightforward transaction: you put

the house up for sale, sell, and split the proceeds. The second option, however, is slightly more complicated.

The decision between the options is a personal one and depends on the couple's specific circumstances. There may be kids who should stay in the house so they can keep friends and school systems; the market may be down, causing a loss on the property that neither party can afford; or one partner can't afford the buy the other partner out.

If you want to buy your partner out, essentially you're refinancing your mortgage using a single income and qualification. Your first step is to ensure you can afford the mortgage payments.

The lender will ask for proof that you're capable of covering the mortgage alone in order for you to apply on your own. In addition to covering the mortgage amount, you'll have to come up with whatever dollar amount you have agreed on to buy your partner out. If you have enough equity in the house, that might be sufficient.

If you can afford the mortgage on your own, the most common means of buying out your partner post-separation and transferring the title out of the joint name and into your own name is to refinance. While the maximum refinance on a home is 80 percent of the appraised value, given the unique circumstances surrounding separation, you can often refinance up to 95 percent of your home's value.

If you're not in a financial position to buy your ex-partner out of the house, and you agree to both stay on the title and have payment arrangements, remember that while one person is responsible for the payments, if the mortgage goes into default, both parties on the mortgage will be affected.

Here, too, mortgage planning is your best friend! If you're informed and prepared, this doesn't need to add to your stress around your divorce.

BREAKING YOUR MORTGAGE

When you break a mortgage early, expect a penalty. Expect, also, that getting your next mortgage will be like doing it all over again. It doesn't matter how many mortgages you've had in the past, or your net worth; you will go through the whole process again. There will be a full review of documents relating to your home's equity, rather than just the down payment review completed with your first mortgage. Lenders will also review your income and current debts, and make a full verification of employment and property approval. You can also count on legal fees.

It's a common mortgage-funding requirement in both

Canada and the US for all of your tax obligations to be paid and up to date. If you're not completely paid up, there are some strategies and solutions we can suggest, but the best lenders will require taxes to be paid.

Equity Take Outs (ETO) are another reason for early mortgage breaks. You might need an ETO for a number of different reasons:

- Do a home renovation (the most common reason)
- Pay education expenses for yourself or your children
- Help your adult kids purchase a home
- Start a business
- Invest in a rental property
- Make dividend-paying investments
- Travel
- Live a more comfortable life

We want to give you control of how to use your resources. We want to empower you to make these decisions based on mortgage planning.

It would be much easier for us to just say, "Take this low rate," all day long. It takes time to educate people. We don't benefit from a client taking a higher rate. We know that if we invest the time—and if you've read this book—you're smart enough to understand we can just skip straight to the place where you benefit from the best mortgage.

A couple in Nanaimo had a good mortgage with us, but their lives were stable and things were going well, and they wanted to see if they could get a better one. Their bank encouraged them to go there for a new mortgage and tempted them with a good rate, so the couple went ahead and took out a mortgage with the bank. They ran into issues, and the person who'd worked with them on the mortgage was—surprise, surprise—no longer with the bank. They learned the hard way their particular mortgage was one they couldn't get out of until the property was sold. They couldn't refinance their debts and they didn't want to sell. The husband's health had declined after surgery, so they wanted to modify the house to accommodate his mobility, only to find they had to take on additional debt because they couldn't modify their mortgage.

In this particular case, we were able to help them, but this sort of situation can be discouraging. We don't want to be here to save the day after the fact; we don't want to see anyone get into that position in the first place.

Just because we placed you with a lender, always come back to us for unbiased advice: don't forget that we're always going to get you the best advice available. We represent you, not the lender, and this one isn't a marriage we take for granted!

CHAPTER ELEVEN

DOWNSIZING, HELPING YOUR KIDS, BUYING INVESTMENT PROPERTIES, AND USING YOUR EQUITY

Why is it so important to be proactive with your mortgage?

The reasons are many, and they focus largely on family and life balance. For the most part, you don't understand how your mortgage can help until you've learned about it, and you don't want to learn too late. It is so unfortunate when we see people who have retired, people who have pride in paying off their mortgages, but who are struggling financially because they didn't know how to leverage the mortgage to help them live a better and more comfortable life.

Paying off your mortgage completely used to be everybody's goal; "pay it and burn it," as the expression went. But think about it: leaving all that tax-free money sitting there doing nothing is like never using the fancy china you got for your wedding. If you don't use it, there's no value in having it.

THE DOWNSIZING DEBACLE

If you've worked hard to pay off your home, now's the time to get your home working for you. What investments can generate cash flow and income opportunities? How can you set yourself up to have these opportunities in the first place? Be proactive and adapt. You will likely have different mortgages for different stages in your life. For example, when you're nearing the end of your mortgage payments, you can look at how to use your equity to generate income. Some people use it to buy stock and make other investments; some people learn about day trading. The best way I know to do it is through rental properties.

These types of properties increase in value, and the tenants make your payments. One day down the road, you'll own the property and you can use its equity to buy more investments. It gives you the freedom to live a life you're comfortable with. I prefer real estate investments, but I maintain a balanced approach: I've always had my eyes and my heart open for opportunities as they come along. Several of my clients have followed suit.

Other people seem to want to complicate things. I had a client who wanted to buy a rental, planning to wait to refinance their principal residence until they found the rental. That's the wrong approach: all it does is add avoidable extra layers of stress and complication to the process. Mortgage rules change constantly; it's why we offer focused assistance in keeping control of your funds and property equity. If you're serious about buying a place, then go ahead and buy it by having your money ready. You can count on us to get that money back if it doesn't go through.

The best way to keep control and remain empowered is to take advantage of every opportunity presented to you. For example, when you take equity out for investment, plan to take out every bit you can qualify for. You can always re-invest back into your mortgage or consider other investment opportunities.

You can also restructure a mortgage into one allowing you to buy before you sell. As we've seen, once you list your property, you no longer qualify for the same products and no lender wants to redo the mortgage on a property that could be sold soon. It isn't attractive for a bank or other lender to invest a great deal of time and money to get you a short-term mortgage that will be paid out before the ink fully dries.

This happens with a lot of people who are downsizing. We get two calls a week from people who think because right now they own a luxury home it'll be easy for them to downsize. Getting a mortgage is still a complex process. It doesn't matter that you already own a place. The rules are the same: put your financial house in order before getting excited about moving into your dream house. With a little foresight and creativity, for example, perhaps you could keep your original property as a rental and generate some extra monthly income.

You don't have to be wealthy or a high-volume real estate investor to do this. This isn't the only way to leverage mortgages, but people who have successfully built ample wealth use real estate as a cornerstone of their financial plans.

INVESTING IN YOUR KIDS' FINANCIAL FUTURE

It's not easy for anyone just starting out to finance their first home. It's common for parents to want to help their kids get started, and there are a couple of ways they can do that. More often than not, when a family's kids start looking into homes, the parents consider two options: becoming a cosigner or helping with the down payment.

DOWN PAYMENT OPTIONS

As we've seen, you're better off giving a down payment as a gift or as an early wealth transfer. Locking in as a cosigner can limit your own future financial options. Also, if you have more than one child, it isn't likely you will qualify to be guarantor on both, so you'll have to do something different for each child. Aside from the stress inherent in this type of scenario, it is typically not the most financially beneficial. There will come a time when a parent is called on to cosign due to credit or income variables, but the best overall option is gifting funds.

As a parent, you should decide whether the money is a legitimate gift, or whether you're expecting repayment. Lenders need to know if it is indeed a gift. If so, they won't use a form of repayment in their calculations. If you expect the money back, they will set it up as a loan and the child (borrower) will qualify for less.

Be prepared to show your bank statements proving where the money came from, and if it hasn't been in an account for ninety days, expect even more paperwork. If the money is from an inheritance, for example, you'll need to provide all the paperwork involved, including copies of the cheque going into the trust account and from the trust account to you. Lenders will require every piece of the puzzle to be verified. If you're gifting money, it's also important to refrain from transferring it back and forth between accounts. Use the information we've been talking about throughout this book; use your common sense; keep it simple.

RENT INVESTMENT PROPERTY OR SELL YOUR HOME TO YOUR KIDS

Some parents decide to do a private sale to their children once the children demonstrate they are financially and emotionally prepared for it, renting the property to them in the meantime. Others downsize and sell their original home to their kids. Those decisions depend on your family dynamics and logistics.

We've seen a lot of financially creative and successful strategies. Some families want to keep everyone close and, even as grandchildren arrive, they all live as one household, modifying the home to fit their generational needs. When the parents age, they move into a condo, leaving the family home to children and grandchildren. These families just do a string of property switches and it works. Besides being efficient, it's a gratifying scenario to witness, as family is one of the most important core values to many Canadians.

INVEST IN YOUR CHILDREN'S BUSINESS

We have many clients who've invested in one or more of their children's business endeavours. One couple helped a child finance his chiropractic education and then rented office space for him when he graduated. Commercial rentals are terribly expensive, and so we recommended buying a space. It takes a few years for a new business to stabilize, and in this case, his earnings weren't as high as expected three years in, and the parents decided to invest in the practice itself, refinance the down payment, and structure the loan that way instead of losing money on rent.

This happens a lot for parents of professional people, like young lawyers, doctors, dentists, veterinarians; the list goes on. It's expensive to start a new practice or business and many parents are willing to help in some way.

Franchises are another example of parent-child financial partnerships, because a great deal of money is required to secure most franchises. Let's look at a fitness franchise as an example. We had a client who needed $800,000 to get a facility built to meet franchise requirements. Her parents believed in it and offered to get a line of credit and a mortgage to help get the franchise up and running. Most franchise models are built with some transparency as to when an investor can begin to see a return, so the parents felt comfortable with the plan. It turned out to be a solid investment.

Parents can be extremely helpful in launching their children's investments or careers. We're always ready to help with advice and strategy when people reach these turning points in their lives and by no means are we suggesting that you're in any way obligated to do this as a parent. We're just sharing our experience with other people's strategies, but we will honour whatever strategy you want to put in place for yourself.

CHAPTER TWELVE

PURCHASING YOUR FIRST HOME

The bulk of our business is with refinancing and renewing existing mortgages, but we also help a substantial number of clients get into their first home, and we understand that situation comes with its own set of stresses and anxieties.

Purchasing a new home involves a lot of work and raises many complicated questions, particularly around what exactly needs to happen and when. To give you some clarity, I divide the process into three stages: preapproval, submission, and file complete.

You'll need to contact us to evaluate your credit and income to see what you can qualify for and how we can position you best. Your income, credit, and down payment are the main components reviewed and an ample subject period is required if you need financing. Remember it's not until due diligence is completed and the property is included in the equation that the lender will provide their options.

PREAPPROVAL

Preapproval is obviously an important first step. This is when we review credit for any outstanding issues through a credit application and income confirmation documents and check in about your down payment. Sometimes this first step flags problems immediately, and we can set to work on improving your situation right away.

Many lenders focus on so-called instant preapprovals. "Click here and get a preapproval in sixty seconds." As we saw earlier, there isn't much profit for a lender in doing a preapproval, as such a low percentage of them actually go through. And there is no legitimate instant preapproval. Some Canadian lenders won't do preapprovals at all. We prefer to spend our time with people who are serious about reviewing their options while moving forward. Not only that, but the same people who clicked or called for the instant preapproval eventually call us anyway, to work with real humans who help them fully understand the credit review and how to move into the best financial position.

Since this is your first mortgage, it's important you remember everything has a shelf life. Everything we ask for is specific to the strategy. Things are always changing, things are always moving, but what stays the same is the need for mortgage intelligence that will weather the storms, the market ups and downs, the regulatory changes, and the sheer unpredictability of life.

The market is a moving target and procrastinating breeds stress and failure.

SUBMISSIONS FOR CONDITIONAL APPROVAL

Once an offer is accepted, you may be required to provide updated documentation. All kinds of things happen with timing, and that's why we do an analysis of your credit, your income, and your down payment. The property in question might also need to be approved. Some documents just won't be available at this stage in the process. Your down payment, for example, must show a full ninety-day history of where the money is coming from. You won't receive funds from your registered retirement savings plans until your offer is accepted.

This is the point in the process when lenders begin their due diligence. They also have the right to request any additional documentation they deem necessary, depending on the buyer's qualifications and property details. If you've submitted anything that doesn't meet compliance, you need to expect some delays. We have a system in place and we'll be following up, but you also have to be on top of the process and not just leave it to us. If you go to someone's house for a dinner party and you haven't let them know about your gluten sensitivity, then you'll probably leave that dinner party hungry and frustrated! Your allergy came as a total surprise to your dinner party host.

Letting people know in advance what to expect is always helpful. Talk to your human resources department about what we'll be needing from them, so it doesn't come as a surprise.

FILE COMPLETE

At this stage, all of the lender's conditions have been satisfied and no further documentation or information is required. Congratulations!

It is now up to the lawyer/notary and client to remove their subject to financing. Remember, the lender might decide to do a final audit of your application prior to completion to verify any changes with the property, income, or down payment. Lenders also retain the right to retract their approval, pending any inconsistencies.

We take pride in being your concierge through this process, and we remain passionate about working together to help you reach your goals, whether this is your first home or your tenth.

AN AMPLE SUBJECT PERIOD

Ample subject period time is critical if you need financing. In spite of the cut-and-dried nature of this component, some people don't seem to understand or accept it. We have a client who's putting 5 percent down on a twenty-six-year-old building, and she and her realtors continue to ask if they can go with a no subject to financing. We have told her numerous times this is a bad idea. If a borrower ever goes into a transaction with a no subject to financing, they are responsible for anything that happens. Obviously, if you meet a lender's parameters, you would expect to be approved. But lenders can pull approval at any time and we have no control over their decisions.

Let's say your credit score has dropped since they held their rate for you, or your job has changed. Maybe the lender isn't keen on the property, or you're willing to pay more for the property than what the lender is willing to offer. They always have the right to decline the opportunity to finance.

In addition, strata documents can be lengthy to process and it's possible the lender doesn't like something about the direction the strata council/condo association is taking, or maybe they need additional documents. Nine out of ten times, it can be done very efficiently, but it's always when you need it done quickly that something comes up.

There are more than thirty people involved in a mortgage transaction. That's a lot of chefs in the kitchen! One might go on holiday and the other one doesn't know where the file is or needs authorization from someone else. Don't forget about real estate agents who might or might not have all the required documents for the property because the sellers are on vacation or reside in another country.

When you get a mortgage approval, you then have to arrange to sign off on it. From there, the lender starts their process of reviewing thousands of pages of documents in order to present everything properly.

Keep your seat belt fastened at all times. The process is complicated and changing. Move quickly when you need to. Don't delay when we ask for information. Those are simple pieces of advice that will make your life much easier. As mortgage brokers, we are an intermediary between you and the lender. We will tell you, yes, the lender said it's a go, but they can still change course. It doesn't happen often, but it happens.

The reality is if you need money for a purchase, the only

way to avoid no subject to financing is to have a 100 percent down payment.

1̲0̲0̲

If you have that kind of money, you probably don't need a mortgage for the purchase! If there's an advantage to acquiring the property quickly, we can refinance later when we don't have time constraints. It's worth noting that the wealthiest people don't pay for their property purchases outright if they can avoid it. My work as a contributor on *Point2 Homes* and seeing firsthand what our wealthiest clients do has taught me that they do things differently. They get the largest mortgage they can!

Remember, if you need someone else's money, understand you will have to modify and work collaboratively with those around you to make it happen. Things can go far more smoothly if you work with someone who has a lot of experience; it can still be a rocky ride, but you can get there safely.

If you take away just one nugget of advice from this chapter, be sure it is this one: the people arranging this for you are not in control of everything. It's like saying a real estate agent can control a seller, or I can control a bank.

Come to the table prepared to work collaboratively and follow our lead. We will take you there.

ELEVATING YOUR MORTGAGE

CHAPTER THIRTEEN

INSURANCE AND TAXES

There are mistakes that can sabotage your mortgage funding, and one of them is not carrying insurance. Insurance is an absolute requirement for every mortgage holder.

MORTGAGE INSURANCE

Let's start with mortgage insurance. As we discussed before, I believe it's critical to have life and disability insurance in place the moment you leave our office. It's not mandatory, but it's the smart and right thing to do. It's pretty simple: if you can't afford the insurance, you can't afford to buy a home. Having home insurance is a condition of funding, so nothing happens without it. It's not possible to secure home insurance after the mortgage, so be prepared ahead of time.

- **High-ratio insurance**: There are a couple of types of

mortgage insurance you might need. One is insurance required if you're putting down less than a 20 percent down payment. Lenders also carry related products to insure on the back end to run their businesses efficiently and provide better offers to customers.

- **Low-ratio insurance:** You won't necessarily be aware of them, but you'll still need to abide by their rules in terms of qualification and credit. At any loan-to-value ratio you can be subject to an insurance (or lender) fee, an amount you pay on top of the mortgage but included in it, which varies depending on a number of factors. If you're a high-ratio borrower, it comes with one particular set of insurance requirements. Lenders may do private insurance, and you'll have to deal with their insurance premiums. Or you may be dealing with a lender with access to a pool of funds, in which case you'll be subject to insurance guidelines but you won't be paying an insurance premium. All of these considerations will play a role in your mortgage, your mortgage rate, your mortgage options, and your mortgage qualification process.

Sometimes, people got mortgage insurance in the past and don't know whether it's still valid. Quite honestly, this is where some lenders don't even know how to save you money! If you walk into a bank with an existing mortgage and you want a new mortgage, the lender will charge you a new insurance premium. They can do so because most people don't know to ask the right questions. But if you qualify, you can port your insurance premium so you don't have to get a new policy and pay all over again. On a $300,000 mortgage, this could save you up to $10,000.

To put this concept in perspective, how long would it take you to earn that much money?

LIFE AND DISABILITY INSURANCE

The other insurance you'll need, as I mentioned, is life and disability insurance. What you need is a life and disability insurance policy independent of your lender, so it can follow you should you change lenders.

This reminds me of Peter and Wendy, who wanted to switch their mortgage with us to a better provider and they couldn't, because they'd taken lender-direct insurance; they'd had health issues throughout the term of the mortgage and so couldn't qualify now with a new provider: they were stuck with a lender that didn't suit their needs. It doesn't matter how young you are (although it's considerably cheaper to buy this kind of insurance when you *are* young), or if you're covered through your employer. You will always have expenses beyond your mortgage, and injury or illness can affect your ability to pay everything.

When you apply for a mortgage, you are legally required

to accept or decline life and disability insurance. Your first priority should be disability insurance, as statistically you're more likely to be injured than you are to die.

People typically assume they're adequately covered through their employer's insurance, whereas the reality is you're only covered to a certain percentage of your income (typically 60 percent). No matter what your income level, 60 percent isn't enough to cover catastrophe.

Disability insurance is the most common coverage people take out to help stem the tide of expenses. If something happens to you, your mortgage and work benefits are covered for up to two years. After reviewing your options with a licensed agent to ensure you have the best product and strategy in place, take advantage of the sixty-day window in which the coverage is free. Where your health and well-being are involved, it is always in your best interest to be covered.

Ask yourself the hard questions. If something happens to you, who is going to care for your children? Who will cook for you, clean your house? At a minimum, you'll require daycare and outside help to manage the home. Who will pay for it?

We all know it's just when you think you have total control over your life that the unexpected can happen. If something happens to you, there's nothing more stressful for your loved ones; don't make a bad crisis worse by putting them in a precarious financial position. Many people never recover financially from accidents and illnesses simply because they never thought it would happen to them.

My agency has seen terrible things happen when people didn't take these elementary precautions. A couple was set to buy a house, and two weeks before taking possession, the husband died of a heart attack. Since both incomes were used to buy the property, the wife found herself in a very challenging financial position. In other cases, some people thought they would be fine, money-wise, if their spouse passed on. Even if both spouses are not working, all home- and child-related expenses must be considered. Ask yourself if you would be 100 percent financially secure without your spouse's income or familial support.

The same goes for property insurance, which is also one of the conditions for getting a mortgage. No mortgage company will lend you money for an uninsured property. You secure the insurance after you sign papers with your mortgage broker and before you go to see a lawyer; we can suggest some for you. To make this process as easy as possible, when you apply for a mortgage with our office, we automatically apply for life, disability, and property insurance on your behalf so everything is ready when needed. You can decide which policies you need to match your situation.

For example, some people who live in condos, or in a strata, choose not to take contents insurance, because the lender essentially gets the coverage they need from the strata in the event of loss. Again, my opinion is if you can't afford contents insurance for your personal items, then you can't afford a mortgage. If your toaster blows a fuse and starts a fire, you'll be on the hook for the strata deductible.

One of our clients lived in a strata and had a house fire: the electric cord on their deep-freeze malfunctioned and started the fire, which—thankfully—was contained before the entire place burned down. This client was fully covered with property insurance. Had they not been covered, they would have been responsible for several substantial fees and would have had to use savings or incur debt to pay them.

Significant renovations also require upgraded home insurance to protect your investment, so make sure that you get your insurance reviewed every year to make sure you have the coverage you need.

Finally, there is title insurance. Title insurance is a form of indemnity insurance (predominantly found in the United States but also in Canada) that insures against financial loss from defects in title to real property as well as from the invalidity or unenforceability of mortgage loans. There are two types of title insurance, one for the lender and one for the borrower. If you're unsure about what you need, consult with your lawyer.

The moral of these stories? Always get insurance!

PORTABILITY[6]

We were just talking about insurance portability, and it makes sense to also mention mortgage portability. The most important thing to remember about portable mortgages is they are never guaranteed. It's a great option to have on a mortgage, but only about 0.003 percent of them actually get ported, due to a change in qualifications or modifications in value. In addition, many lenders seem to find ways to deem mortgages ineligible to port.

Generally, if there's modification beyond 10 percent of the original mortgage value, the mortgage is not portable. Many times, homeowners pay down more than 10 percent or need more than 10 percent to move up the property ladder. Depending on how long you've owned your home, you've likely paid down more than 10 percent equity. Some lenders say you only have thirty days to port a mortgage, but a number of factors—the closing date of

6   Mortgage portability does not exist in the United States.

purchase, for example, or of downsizing—will determine whether or not you qualify.

Depending on the loan-to-value amount, this might place you in a different category due to how that lender structured the product. If the lender no longer has the product, or it doesn't fit in the "bundle" of mortgages financed, then it won't work for you. In other cases, you might not qualify for it today, based on your income or credit. The property itself might not even fit the criteria anymore. For example, we have some lenders offering a really great rate, but it is only for single-family homes, not for condos or townhouses. In that scenario, the homeowner couldn't port their mortgage from the house to a condo.

We look at three Ps with mortgages—penalties, prepayment privileges, and portability. If I had to choose one of the three, it would be the prepayment privileges for their flexibility.

That's the point here: there's a tremendous market variation in terms of what's available and for whom. Taking the time to contact insurance companies to see if you were previously insured can save you $10,000 to $20,000 on average. Some people obtained mortgage insurance five or ten years ago and don't know whether they still have it or if it's still valid.

For example, if you had mortgage insurance on your home

five years ago, you might qualify for better products if you don't make any modifications to the mortgage. Many lenders don't check for that and, depending on how educated the client is, they don't think to ask. We had a client who bought a presale and their new build wasn't going to be ready for six months. They sold their existing home and moved in with family members. Their private banker was only allowed to port the insurance for three months. We saved them $11,000 in premiums right off the top.

My team tries to work with lenders that will give you the longest options to port an increase, provided you qualify. Not everyone qualifies, of course, based on changing situations or timing, but unlike most banks and other lenders, we first look to port your premium. Banks and lenders are trained to charge you again unless you question it and in cases like this, you could save $10,000 on a $300,000 mortgage. That's good news for you, as is the life and disability insurance we can offer, which is independent to you, no matter where you end up. It follows you regardless of which lender you ultimately do business with.

PROPERTY TAXES

Property taxes seem to follow you around like a new puppy. Taxes aren't quite as fun as puppies! But play it smart and you can "teach" them to follow your lead just the same.

The smartest strategy with property taxes? Don't bundle them to pay with your mortgage. Instead of paying a lender, set up an account with your city and in some cases you'll earn a discount.

Don't defer property taxes. If you defer, you will no longer qualify for a mortgage without paying those out first with other funds. It's that simple: lenders will not give you a mortgage with deferred taxes, and usually omit that when you are applying to get that done (another retention strategy?). Many people think, "I can't wait until I'm fifty-five when I can totally defer my property taxes." Hold your horses; it's not all rosy. Just ask Margaret.

Margaret was retiring and wanted to pay off some outside debt. She listened to my radio show and decided to give us a call. She mentioned something about her property taxes being deferred, but what she didn't realize was she couldn't get a new mortgage until she paid them. That kind of deferment puts any borrower into a difficult position. If she had just renewed her mortgage, she would have lost out on $2,400 a month in savings—savings that we were able to provide to her. Because she was changing her property taxes, she had to cash out other investments first to pay those property taxes off. We ended up helping her with a plan to pay the taxes and get into a new mortgage, but the lesson is clear: you can't make modifications to a mortgage unless you pay your property taxes.

Margaret isn't alone. Many people are unaware of property tax variables. There are times when lenders make it mandatory to pay property tax with the mortgage, and they charge you for it, typically on a monthly or yearly basis. Charges generally average $2 to $5 a month, or $100 a year. It may not sound like much, but fees like those will add up quickly.

If lenders offer a lower interest rate but charge a hefty fee to manage the tax, it's another cost you might not have been expecting and it adds to the total borrowing amount. Keep in mind, regardless of whether you pay monthly or annually, the lender only remits payment once a year. The rest of the year they're earning money from your money and all the other property tax accounts in their system. Finally, if all that wasn't enough to convince you, at the end of the day, lenders also can make mistakes, and if they make mistakes with your taxes, you're the one responsible—and liable. Follow the lead of the wealthy, who don't allow themselves to be handcuffed to a particular lender or program. They pay taxes and deploy their equity to consistently earn more money.

If you own twenty properties, and managing them all isn't your thing, or you don't have the time, it might make sense to have the lender handle it. But for the rest of us? Save the money and headache and do it yourself. Go directly to your municipality and set up a preauthorized debit account with them. Some municipalities even offer a discount to pay directly with them. Choosing this option gives you control of the situation. You don't pay a lender to collect the taxes and you don't pay any unnecessary fees.

You have choices on where and how to spend your money, and this one can alleviate a great deal of stress.

CHAPTER FOURTEEN

DON'T SABOTAGE YOUR MORTGAGE FUNDING!

You want a mortgage. We want you to have a mortgage. In the best of all possible worlds we'll be working together to get you funding you can live with that will boost your finances and enable you to move up the property ladder.

But only if you don't sabotage it.

Too many clients think once they've been approved, everything is fine and they can relax completely. That's just not the way it works. At various times between the first approval and the closing, both my team and the lender are going to do a full look back on all your finances, your life situation, everything that went into your application. If you have any changes to make in your life and you've already been approved, wait until your mortgage is funded before doing anything that could possibly change your status.

DON'T CHANGE YOUR MIND

Once you've been approved, you need to consider your application as being written in stone. If you believe your home inspection, for example, didn't quite live up to expectations, you can't go back to the lender and try to renegotiate your mortgage. Nothing will kill the deal faster, and nothing will create more questions about you for your lender.

The lender needs to be reassured that you're still a great candidate for a mortgage loan, which isn't going to happen if you try to change the terms midway through the process. Once your financial snapshot is in place, what you want to do is stay as close to it as you possibly can.

We've seen people do all sorts of things at the last minute. Sometimes they try to change the date for the funding. Sometimes they decide to change lawyers. If you feel anything needs adjustment, it's essential you tell us about it first, so we can advise you on the best course of action. Otherwise you're just sabotaging your own best chances for success.

BEST WAYS TO QUASH YOUR APPROVAL

Your purchase or refinance completion can be jeopardized by a number of different factors. Here are some do's and don'ts for making sure you don't give yourself (or your lender) any negative surprises. We actually send this out during the application process to our clients:

- Don't change employers, jobs, or income, even if you're anticipating a raise; wait until after your application has been funded.
- Don't apply for any new credit cards or for anything involving a credit check. Lenders always reserve the right to pull another credit check before closing if they want to, and if your score has gone down they could easily pull their approval.
- Don't take on any additional debt. We've seen people buy major appliances or even vehicles on credit between the time of their application and their funding. This changes your entire debt-to-income ratio, and not in a good way.
- Don't close out any active accounts. In fact, don't move any money around. Depending on how you're getting your down payment, or where the equity is coming from, lenders might need a last-minute copy of a bank statement. Keep in mind that anything can be scrutinized during this period, so you want to stay financially clean.
- Don't get into any disputes that could result in collec-

tions (in other words, pay your parking tickets, pay your hydro bills, pay your credit cards). People fight on principle all the time. They even say, "It's the principle of the thing." That principle is only going to take you so far and it can end up really impacting your finances.

- Don't schedule a vacation leading up to the date of your completion of your mortgage. Lenders and lawyers can request things at the last minute that you will be required to provide or handle. This is something that happens more frequently than you'd imagine, and I guarantee if you go on vacation, something will come up. Save the vacation for celebration later. You're needed here, now.

- Do disclose the shape of your selected property upfront. It's not a good idea to have your home gutted or extensive renovations performed and expect an appraiser or lender won't notice or won't mind. It will impact both your valuation and your approval.

- As we saw above, never make last-minute changes to anything: to the amount, to the date, or to the term. This is the biggest way to cause a problem. It is a big deal to get everything through all the steps needed to approve these changes. All conditions must be met ten business days before your completion date. Changing anything can add to the interest cost.

- Do make sure your initial application is correct. People get married or get divorced and change their name or forget they had a cosigner on their mortgage. If you've had a name change, make sure you have all the appropriate documentation, because there could be inconsistencies that will be questioned. If you've ever had a name change, make sure you have documentation of it: the presence of aliases can be an issue for compliance.

The client going away on vacation before closing is the most common scenario we see with respect to self-sabotage. We had one situation in which the client was getting part of the proceeds for their purchase from an inheritance. We needed a copy of the will; we needed a copy of the Statement of Adjustment showing what money went where; we needed a copy of the money going into the trust account and then from the trust account into the bank account. All sorts of detailed documentation was required, and the client disappeared. They went on vacation. They were unreachable. Then when they were reachable, of course they didn't want to be concerned about these documents.

You can imagine what happened to their mortgage: lots of unnecessary temporary stress.

CHAPTER FIFTEEN

YOUR LAWYER'S ROLE IN YOUR MORTGAGE

Before we explore the roles of lawyers in the mortgage process, it should be noted that most of the information in this chapter applies primarily to Canada. In the United States, a title company does most of the work that falls under the Canadian lawyer's purview. In the United States, you will need a lawyer to handle your closing, but not to secure your mortgage.

The term "escrow" used in the United States refers to the process of the title company facilitating the real estate transaction. After the buyer and seller provide the title company with the contract, written instructions, documents, and funds, escrow is opened. The escrow officer makes sure the closing goes smoothly and everyone gets paid what they're owed. After the closing, the escrow agent records the deed and title transfer that make the home officially yours.

When you decided to register your mortgage with a lawyer, it became their responsibility to follow through. We are not law specialists, of course, but we have years of experience working with the best (and less than best) firms in Canada.

A lawyer is the one responsible for explaining what your closing costs will be. They will know the intricacies involved along with any updated legislation or grants, and you need to work collaboratively with your lawyer to be sure you are protected. You might think that because your lawyer "does this all day long," you can sit back with no worries. The reality is, lawyers do all kinds of things all day long. (Yes, speaking of which, this is a good time to create or revise a will!) We can make recommendations on what to discuss, but most importantly, you should put together a checklist of questions and concerns ahead of time, which should include:

- How should I be registering the property most beneficial to estate planning?
- Are there any grants available based on my life stage and mortgage financing? (This question will trigger a lawyer to ask about your goal and what the money is for. From there, they can work with you through the application process or simply remind you the option is there.)

However, keep in mind that your lawyer's focus is to register the title, advise you on matters related to that process, and confirm that everything matches the mortgage instructions. They're not there to comment on any mortgage specifics. Lawyers are not specialists in understanding the differences between lenders. Lawyers get confused as much as you or I do when two lenders have different costs, or the same verbiage but totally different policies in their penalties!

When we do a mortgage for a client, we ask them which lawyer they plan to use, per our recommendations or otherwise. Some lawyers are very good at what they do, and others are terrible.

They generally do the best they can. What we do on our end to ensure everything is done in the most efficient manner is send all relevant documents to the lawyer in advance. This includes an introduction to you, along with all necessary information related to the transaction. From there, the lawyer knows to contact us with any questions to effectively and efficiently complete your file.

Some lawyers are horrible. It's as simple as that. Some don't acknowledge client introduction, call at the last minute, or ask clients to come in multiple times. In their defence—no pun intended—with more than one hundred different lenders out there, it's generally impossible for every lawyer to fully understand all the different sets of lender rules. That's a big reason why we send the documents off to the lawyer as soon as a lender has signed off on our conditions. That way, clients can gauge a lawyer's reliability and integrity through return correspondence right off the bat.

A good lawyer responds right away with some sort of confirmation. "Thank you so much. Here's our next step with the file." The ones we have problems with are those who don't reply. They "ghost," and then the day before closing, a client might call in a panic, saying the lawyer contacted them for more information, or a condition was not signed off, and now the client has to rush in to sign something. In some cases, the lawyer never contacted the client at all and things were not being done on time. To avert disaster, we had to go elsewhere.

In related but non-legal matters, such as renewals with no title changes, clients can use a title company. They have programs with many of the banks, and they'll send a representative to witness your signatures and ID. They can only be used for refinances and for switches with an existing mortgage, however. They aren't authorized to give any legal advice on how a mortgage is registered among borrowers, or to assist with grants, anything that is available provincially, or any type of planning advice.

LAWYERS AREN'T INFALLIBLE

We're all human, and humans make mistakes. Put aside your lawyer jokes for a minute; they are tasked with a great many details and constantly changing rules. Mistakes happen. A solid lawyer will catch mistakes before they come around, or quickly put out the fire to the best of their ability. Lawyers a few steps down the ladder might not be so adept.

An avoidable blunder on the part of a lawyer forced a client of ours to take a mortgage forty points higher than needed.

There are two ways to register a mortgage: it can be a running account or a single charge. The way a mortgage is registered determines the client's options at renewal, so it's critical the whole deal fires on all cylinders. We want clients to happily move into their new home, without a wave of document despair. The client's lender in this example had instructions to only run the mortgage as a single charge. This means at the end of the term, the client can go anywhere else to get their mortgage done, generally with no legal fees. (If it's registered as a running account, in most cases clients have to do a full refinance with new legal fees.)

The lawyer screwed up—there's no other way to say it—on how they registered the paperwork, and they sent the wrong form. We tried contacting the lawyer to no avail.

The lawyer was, for all intents and purposes, invisible, and didn't make the change we needed. We knew the lender didn't register running mortgages, so the client was stuck renewing with their existing bank, even though they'd qualified for a better mortgage with a monoline lender.

This entire disaster was totally on the lawyer. We did our part and obviously cannot micromanage the process. In the end, we were not able to help the client get the mortgage due to the paperwork error.

Some of the problem falls on the traditional makeup of a law firm. You have to remember it's lawyers' associates, not the lawyers themselves, who actually do most of the paperwork. For the most part in mortgage processes, the lawyers don't know much of anything about the file. The scene sometimes plays out like this: lawyer walks in and says, "Do you have any questions? Okay, I'll check that out for you." It's the associates who actually do all the work, and do they triple-check the correct box has been ticked? Apparently, not always! In addition, you need to remember that the lawyer is part of your team, and you need to work collaboratively with them to get the job done.

Don't get me wrong; I'm not bashing lawyers. Many of them do fantastic work, but there are a lot of mechanics involved and, every now and then, someone loses a part.

Of course, we always do whatever we can to help. Much is dependent on the quality and experience of your lawyer. They are, after all, the last person to sign the documents.

We can look at a few examples to illustrate the importance of staying aware of the details. To start with, payments we set up aren't reflected on the commitment; they are reflected in our office after the fact. If you're eligible for any grants or tax benefits, it's the lawyer's responsibility to review them with you. They're also responsible to review final outstanding debt on credit cards when we enter into debt consolidation.

We have systems in place to minimize problems, but it is still a collaborative process that benefits from open communication and positive relations among all parties involved.

What items should you, as the borrower, cover with your lawyer? Check to make sure your lawyer understands their responsibilities, which include:

- The pros and cons of the different ways of registration available (so you get the best choice)
- Your qualifications for first-time homebuyers' grants
- Any other tax rebates available
- Addition of spouses on previously owned properties and any subsequent taxes

- Independent legal advice
- Spousal consent

In our office, we do everything possible to ensure the process with lawyers goes smoothly. When we get a completed file from a lender, we don't just count on everything being fine. We send all our paperwork to the lawyer and tell them to contact us if they have any questions prior to the client coming in. We then follow up further to confirm they have no questions and have made an appointment with the borrower. Not all lawyers have experience with all lenders, and they don't all understand the nuances of why a specific lender and terms were selected. Their job is to register title and advise on the grants and tax/cost implications of each way.

CONCLUSION

I like to think of this point in the book as a call to action rather than a conclusion. We're only just beginning. If I've done my part, you are confident you won't find a better experience with any other mortgage broker. Until we meet to plan your bright future, I will leave you with a few final thoughts on the mortgage world and my passion to bring you the best of it.

Now that you've understood the "why" of the process, you're ready to proceed directly with action. This book doesn't include every piece of information you need; my goal is to help you access that information and understand why you need it. In other words, what I have been trying to help you understand is how to evaluate the best mortgage. We will be the constant in change to help you navigate the market.

We discussed earlier some of the common mistakes people make with mortgages. The most significant and common mistake is a general lack of understanding of mortgages, how they are reviewed, and how funding is done behind the scenes—in other words, poor mortgage intelligence. Consumers tend to think they should be able to get a great mortgage at a great rate with a minimum of fuss and not a lot of work on their part.

That's not reality.

Banks and lenders in general do not have your best interests in mind. By not taking the initiative, you're inviting crises into your financial life. That's why I'm so passionate about helping people avoid stressful, costly mistakes and bringing clarity to how mortgages and their related influences will affect individuals' financial wellness. It's my passion that informs everything I do, from consulting on mortgages to working with lenders, insurers, and other partners to ensure our clients are offered the very best options.

That passion translates into continued savings, enhanced opportunities, and an overall sense of well-being for our clients. It also informs the way we treat everybody. We are not the best fit for everyone out there, and if we're not, we're still going to help them find the right way forward for their specific circumstance.

That passion extends to everyone reading this book, because now you have the information you need to align yourself with the very best mortgage professionals in your area if I cannot help you or suggest someone to you, to ask the right questions.

CANADIAN AND US MORTGAGE MARKETS

A lot of millennials want to live a more balanced life. Right now, about 30 percent of baby boomers in Vancouver and Toronto are investing in the United States for second homes. There's a definite trend: people from Toronto generally invest in Florida, while people from British Columbia generally invest in Palm Springs.

People in my age group are asking how they can get their equity working for them. They're wondering how to get that second home, whether it's here or somewhere warm and sunny in the US.

With that in mind, we've helped a lot of Canadians buy real estate in the United States. My husband already owns property in Phoenix, and right now I'm looking for a family home to buy there, something we can rent out but that will also be our second home. My plan is to continue doing what I've done here at home—purchasing more rentals, really establishing myself in the United States.

With all the baby boomers buying second residences in the United States, it's important for Americans to know I'm personally invested in the States myself. And it's important for Canadians to know that if that's one of their goals, we've got that covered. We have a mortgage for that. Not only do we have a mortgage for that, but it's a route we're taking personally.

Just like the lending space in Canada, lending criteria and the market in the United States tend to be localized. If people reach out to me, if I have an associate in that area that I can trust, I'll be able to make an appropriate introduction. I also understand the differences between the Canadian and the American markets, as I've outlined throughout this book, and no matter where you are, in the US or across Canada, just looking at all the loan's components is part of being mortgage savvy.

CONGRATULATIONS YOU'VE UNLOCKED THE CODE!

Everything flows when you follow the correct process, but it has to be collaborative. I like to think of my team working alongside you as one informed, combined force that gets it done. We have the experience and tools to help lead the charge, and we have expectations that the transparency we offer will be a two-way street.

Anything related to a mortgage, credit, income, or if a client has been to another lender or broker, is absolutely relevant to the business part of the transaction. It's important for clients to be transparent about their marital status, financial obligations, and life status, and realize giving their mortgage professional 100 percent will come back to them in like form.

I am a very dynamic player, with my clients as my number-one priority, but I count on those clients to understand their part in the process before and during our partnership. That's true for all top mortgage professionals.

There are times when it is not in a client's best interests to work with us, and we are very upfront when it happens. I believe integrity and honesty are big reasons why people choose to come to us. When you share our core values, the process is seamless, with blue ribbon results.

We can look at a comparison to illustrate these benefits. If you go to a bank, you are there representing nothing other than a sale. With my team, you are evaluated as a partner in a relationship. It isn't possible for a company with one product or one option to offer an unbiased opinion of the best client scenario.

We're here to live the best life we can. Part of living abundantly and fulfilled is doing the best we can with our best abilities every time. In our business, there's no value in floundering in a place where we are not able to help people. There's no value in being dishonest. There are things we can control and things we can't. There are things that are good for people and things that aren't. Our goal is to be straight up with all of it, and be here for you.

It gives me great satisfaction to educate and help people, to open people's eyes to levels they didn't even know existed and mistakes they didn't know they were making. It can often be just a simple change or two that makes the difference. We're not here to reinvent the wheel, but we can continue to improve it when opportunities present themselves. What I'm doing here is opening a book on many closed-door secrets the rest of the financial world doesn't want you to know. When you have this information, you're empowered to get the very best for yourself and your family. It is very comforting to know you can enter a scenario, be completely transparent, and secure the best possible assistance.

I wrote this book essentially as a public service announcement. The more empowered and intelligent decisions people can make, the less reliant they are on things they cannot control and the less likely they are to be taken advantage of. I don't believe any of us wants to rely on our parents' passing or on a government pension to receive money. These days, most of us can't even rely on employers! Change can happen at any time and upset your entire life balance. It's empowering to be self-sufficient and have confidence in the security of knowing you are dealing with the best possible scenario at any given moment. You deserve that, and I've shared insider knowledge to help you obtain it by raising your mortgage intelligence. If I'm honest and helpful, then I feel I am doing my best for you, my community, and my legacy in the world.

I stay focused to ensure that legacy holds true. I believe the psychology of mortgages has been completely wrong for decades and offering my talent and passion has given me the opportunity to be part of a movement to a more empowering society that embraces financial empowerment. One of the biggest struggles facing people all over the world, young and older alike, is the lack of a clear life-goal. I was very fortunate to have a defined path ahead of me, and I followed it to a rewarding career. I liken my story to that of teachers or doctors who choose specific fields to educate, treat, and nurture people to give them the best possible life.

I feel this is my calling: to help people be the best they can be and understand what they can do to get ahead.

I've always found the best ideas in life are the simplest. How many times have you stopped and realized, "That's so simple. Why didn't I think of that?" That's exactly my view on mortgages. It doesn't have to be as complicated a process as many would have you believe. With me as your partner, you will see how easy and productive the process can be. Many people came to us without clarity on exactly what we do and how we sift through the complexities inherent in the mortgage journey. Fast-forward, and thousands of families and individuals live in their dream homes, or have moved up the property ladder, with our help. That is so important to me and it's my legacy in this business—being authentic and executing core values every day.

My place in the community, through awards I've received and services I've provided, is wonderful, but I am equally proud of and grateful for the opportunity to give back to many charitable organizations that include the CKNW Kids' Fund, the Santa Fox Food Drive, and the Eagle Ridge Hospital. I continue to be a tremendous proponent of the #givewhereyoulive concept.

My own journey continues. I was blessed to have great mentors who taught me to understand credit, income, savings, and the truth behind marketing and how to avoid costly mistakes. I had these mentors because I sought them out.

Success always leaves clues behind, and I want to create

a path strewn with clues for others to follow by demonstrating by example.

I'm proud of my accomplishments and thankful to be a positive part of my community, and I continue to build on what makes my team unique. We have seen a great deal of change in the industry and our strength is in our ability to adapt. With every major industry shift, I've succeeded in understanding the impact and applying my understanding to the benefits of our clients. I just really love doing my best! Again, our first priority is taking care of our own family, and then giving others the information they need to apply it to their lives. Our mortgage family, associates, media—and always in that order.

A huge bonus, of course, is the hard work put into our radio show and its subsequent benefit for our clients. *The Mortgage Show* on CKNW is Canada's longest-running radio show dedicated to mortgage issues. Last year was my ninth consecutive contribution to the CKNW Kids' Fund, and I sat down with one of the afternoon hosts to discuss my show's long run. I remember sitting at the microphone only two weeks from having my first baby, and I've brought my kids to the donation event every year since. The host asked how long *The Mortgage Show* had been on the air and was impressed not only with how long the show had been running, but with how it's been renewed an unheard-of ten years in a row. It takes a lot of commitment and, frankly, when you reach this level of success in an industry, some people ask whether you really need to keep doing it anymore.

My answer is yes. I do.

I am fuelled by helping as many people as I can. That's it. It sounds cliché, but this isn't a job for me; it's my passion. Every day, something changes in life, as it does in this industry. I love the challenge and I keep three principles at the forefront of my strategy—Planning, Optimizing, and Protecting. I review them daily to help execute the correct scenario for everyone, which I call my POP strategy, partly for the acronym, and because it's the most POPular approach. I have a great team around me to assist with paperwork (my least favourite chore) and other tasks, and the end reward for me is seeing how clients progress, being a part of the life they're able to create with our help. I always look to do the same thing in my personal life, and when you come from a place of doing it for yourself, it makes it that much more fulfilling to help others get there.

Remember, the only person who has to live with your financial choices is you. Knowing that, you have to take a logical approach in seeking out the mortgage broker who is your best match, and who is passionate about what they do in business and their personal life. When I'm trying to learn more about something, I look to people who are the best in their field, who think strategically, and who execute with passion. If everyone else is going one way, I won't just blindly follow along. I'll ask myself fundamental questions to identify my accountability in the role and a strategy to work together with a client. This elevates my performance, my client's result, and the industry as a whole.

I don't know that everybody has the kind of empathy we have. I don't know that every mortgage broker team is willing to spend the kind of time and energy it takes to get to know their clients as well as we do, or work as hard for them as we do.

I've been doing this since shortly after I graduated high school and I am very grateful to have been recognized for it every step of the way. It's been an amazing journey so far...and the best is yet to come.

Join me on our website for the latest information, media appearances, and to sign up for our newsletter: angelacalla.ca.

ABOUT THE AUTHOR

Since 2004, **ANGELA CALLA** has been passionate about helping borrowers avoid costly mistakes through regional and national media, including as host of CKNW's *The Mortgage Show* and her personal practice as a mortgage broker. She has received numerous awards for excellence in her field and is consistently ranked in the top 1% of mortgage brokers in Canada. When not working, Angela also contributes to her community, spends time with her husband and children, and loves bringing people together to celebrate life's beauty. To contact her, visit angelacalla.ca.

The proceeds from this book are going to various regional charities.

Made in the USA
San Bernardino, CA
26 November 2019

60492602R00178